Steven 08

THE RIGHT TO DEVELOPMENT IN A CLIMATE CONSTRAINED WORLD

Published by the Heinrich Böll Foundation,
Christian Aid, EcoEquity and the Stockholm Environment Institute

Berlin, November 2007

Photos: Surjina from Bangladesh makes a training to become an electrician, Wolfgang Radke/KNA-Bild (title), Christian Aid/Andrew Njoroge Caption (4), dpa (8, 34, 56), Christian Aid/Hannah Morley (14), Christian Aid/Claire Shelley (18), Christian Aid/Mohammadur Rahman (22), Presse- und Informationsamt der Bundesregierung (44), Greenpeace (67)

Layout: graphic syndicat, Michael Pickardt

Printing: agit-druck

ISBN 978-3-927760-71-4

This report can be ordered from:
Heinrich Böll Foundation, Rosenthaler Str. 40/41, 10178 Berlin,
T +49 30 285340 **F** +49 30 28534109 **E** info@boell.de, www.boell.de
www.ecoequity.org/docs/TheGDRsFramework.pdf

HEINRICH BÖLL STIFTUNG
PUBLICATION SERIES ON ECOLOGY

VOLUME 1

The Right to Development in a Climate Constrained World

The Greenhouse Development Rights Framework

A report by Paul Baer and Tom Athanasiou of EcoEquity and Sivan Kartha of the Stockholm Environment Institute, with the support of Christian Aid and the Heinrich-Böll-Foundation

Farmer and mother Damaris Nunda stands on her four acre smallholding having been helped to grow various crops in changeable weather conditions in Kenya thanks to the sustainable advice of Christian Aid-supported organisation, BIDII. (The Benevolent Institute of Development Initiatives)

PREFACE

Imagine a world in which both the scandal of global poverty and the threat of climate change were taken seriously. In such a world, what action would be required to deliver human development, economic opportunity and dignity to poor people while at the same time reducing the atmospheric concentration of greenhouse gases and holding global warming below 2 degrees Celsius?

So constrained is the global carbon budget – global emissions must peak in the next decade and start a precipitous decline between now and 2025 – that it is too late to talk of emissions reductions in Annex 1 countries alone. It is now necessary to secure significant cuts in emissions in the growing nations of the developing world. And yet, even in the burgeoning Chinese and Indian economies, there is till huge poverty. This is the crux of the current climate impasse.

Christian Aid and the Heinrich Boll Foundation are therefore proud to be associated with "The Right to Development in a Climate Constrained World" because it tackles this issue head on. It argues that while people remain poor, it is unacceptable and unrealistic to expect them to focus their valuable resources on the climate change crisis. And it draws the necessary conclusions – that others who are wealthier and have enjoyed higher levels of emissions already, must take on their share of the burden.

To be clear, this does not mean that the countries in which poor people live are not required to cut their emissions, but rather that the global consuming class – the elites both within these countries and in the industrialized countries – are the ones who must pay.

The locus for this idea is the United Nations Framework Convention on Climate Change itself. The Convention states that in tackling climate change countries should respond according to their "...common but differentiated responsibilities and respective capabilities and their social and economic conditions". The Greenhouse Development Rights Framework attempts to work this idea through in a manner that explicitly safeguards the right to development. It lays out and quantifies the burden-sharing framework that would logically follow from clear and defensible measures of responsibility and capability defined so as to preserve developmental equity.

The results are not wholly surprising. One-third of the burden of dealing globally with climate change falls on the shoulders of the US and one-quarter is down to the European Union. The bigger developing nations with a sizable consuming class are net receivers of mitigation finance but still have to add some of their own, and the poorest nations can focus their efforts on achieving sustainable development goals.

Its authors, along with Christian Aid and Heinrich Boll Foundation, will undoubtedly face questions about whether or not this is a politically realistic proposition. After all, the international negotiations are currently in a precarious condition and the essential pre-requisite of any global deal – big cuts in industrialised countries – is far from being universally acknowledged.

Our response is simple: a climate change agreement stands a far greater chance of winning global support if the issue of sustainable human development is in its DNA.

And this can only happen if a fair and adequate global burden sharing architecture that explicitly safeguards the right to development is on the table for all to see. "The Right to Development in a Climate Constrained World" fills that gap, and so it is without apology that we advance it as an opening salvo in a new round of debate on precisely how this might be done. Our only caveat is that we must move forward with renewed urgency as we have very little time to stop crisis becoming catastrophe.

Christian Aid and the Heinrich Boll Foundation would like to offer profound thanks to Paul Baer and Tom Athanasiou of EcoEquity and Sivan Kartha of the Stockholm Environment Institute for devising, writing, refining and being willing to take on board any number of suggestions and comments en route to publishing this document.

Barbara Unmüßig
Member of the Executive Board
Heinrich-Böll-Stiftung

Dr Daleep Mukarji
Director
Christian Aid

TABLE OF CONTENTS

A Maasai women dances while holding a banner saying "Stop climate injustice" at a demonstration in Nairobi, Kenya, on Saturday 11 November, 2006. More than 5.000 people braved the rain to march in support of initiatives to combat global warming, the first of its kind to be held in Africa, to coincide with the United Nations Climate Change Conference being held in the country until 17 November.

The Right to Development in a Climate Constrained World

The Greenhouse Development Rights Framework*

Abstract

This paper argues that an emergency climate program is needed, that such a program is only possible if the international climate policy impasse is broken, and that this impasse arises from the inherent – but surmountable – conflict between the climate crisis and the development crisis. It argues that the best way to break this impasse is, perhaps counter-intuitively, by expanding the climate protection agenda to include the protection of developmental equity. To that end, the Greenhouse Development Rights (GDRs) framework is designed to hold global warming below 2°C while, with equal deliberateness, safeguarding the right of all people everywhere to reach a dignified level of sustainable human development. We present in this paper an exposition of the GDRs framework and indicative quantification of its implications.

Executive Summary

Climate science tells us that we have pushed beyond "dangerous anthropogenic interference with the climate system," and are on the verge of committing to catastrophic interference. In this context, it is necessary to raise our heads, if only for a moment, from the tactical scrum, and to consider brute necessity. To that end, we argue for a stringent mitigation pathway (one that can only be achieved by way of an international emergency program) that would give us a reasonable probability of keeping global warming below 2°C. This implies a pathway that would have global emissions peak in 2015 and then drop at a resolute 6 percent per year, to reach a level of 80 percent below 1990 levels in 2050. Along the way, CO_2 concentrations would peak near 425 ppm (with CO_2-equivalent levels reaching about 470 ppm) before they begin to fall.

---

* The principal authors of this report are Paul Baer and Tom Athanasiou of EcoEquity and Sivan Kartha of the Stockholm Environment Institute. Please cite as: Baer, P., T. Athanasiou and S. Kartha. 2007. "The Right to Development in a Climate Constrained World: The Greenhouse Development Rights Framework" (www.ecoequity.org/GDRs). This paper is very slightly revised from the previous version published online on September 24, 2007. Address correspondence to GDRs@ecoequity.org.

Such an emergency pathway is, to be sure, a technical challenge; but it is even more a political challenge. After all, the defining political reality of the climate crisis is that we confront it within a profoundly and bitterly divided world characterized by staggering levels of poverty amid enormous (and growing) wealth. And while the usual path from poverty to prosperity is via a development process that entails dramatic increases in the per capita use of fossil fuel energy, this path must be closed. Any future in which it is taken by even a significant fraction of the world's poor is a future in which dramatically rising carbon emissions make a mockery of emergency rhetoric.

This leads us, inevitably, to the intersection of the climate crisis and the development crisis, and to the core of the climate challenge: The world's wealthy minority has left precious little atmospheric space for the poor majority. Indeed, it has left so little space that, even if industrialized country emissions were to be suddenly and magically halted, the dramatic emissions reduction demanded by the climate crisis would require the developing countries to urgently decarbonize their economies, and to do so while they are still combating endemic poverty. This is not only the core of the physical challenge, but also the crux of the international political impasse that now stymies the negotiations.

If an emergency program is to have any hope of being embraced, we must take care that it does not threaten to lock in today's vast disparities of wealth and income. Just the contrary: It must drive down emissions, globally, even while the lives of the poor are improving and ambitious development goals are being met and surpassed. To this end, it must slash the emissions of the already wealthy and, at the same time, prevent the unbounded emissions growth of those rising out of poverty. And it must do so without stifling their development aspirations.

The problem, of course, is that the world's wealthier citizens will not at present agree to pay more than a trivial amount for climate change, and even less if the payments go to people and projects in "other countries". Given this, southern negotiators can be forgiven if they fear that a stringent global climate agreement would wind up saddling them with unacceptable costs and permanently constraining their development. In any case, poor countries, if they see mitigation as drawing resources from development and poverty alleviation, will balk at it. Which is why, before finally throwing their support behind any emergency program, southern negotiators will need to see a proposal that, above all else, explicitly safeguards the right to development.

Thus, the political impasse. As long as there is no serious burden-sharing proposal on the table, one that ensures that an emergency program can be executed without stifling development in the South, developing-country negotiators will conclude that their countries have more to lose than to gain from earnest engagement. In this context, we offer "Greenhouse Development Rights" as a reference burden-sharing framework for a regime that could break the impasse.

The GDRs framework seeks to not only acknowledge the right to development but to actually place that right at its structural core. It seeks to secure for the developing nations a viable portion of the scant remaining atmospheric space, and to do so in a manner that allows them to prosper within it. It does this by codifying the right to development in terms of a development threshold, below which individuals are not required to help shoulder the burden of solving the climate problem. This development threshold is defined to reflect a level of welfare beyond basic needs, but well short of today's levels of "affluent" consumption, which is to say that people below it have little responsibility for the climate problem and relatively little capacity to invest in solving it. Indeed, they have development as their proper priority, and as they struggle toward a viable level of social well-being, they cannot reasonably be saddled with the costs of keeping society as a whole within the starkly limited global carbon budget.

People above the development threshold, on the other hand, are taken as having realized their right to development, and as bearing the responsibility to preserve that right for others. It is they who must share the burden – in accordance with the UNFCCC's broad principle of "common but differentiated responsibility and respective capabilities" – of funding the global emergency program. It is they who must bear the costs of not only curbing the emissions associated with their own consumption, but also of ensuring that, as those below the threshold rise toward and then above it, they are able to do so along sustainable, low-emission paths.

In all this, responsibility and capacity are not mere pretty words, repeated here because they are prominently featured in the Framework Convention. Rather, they are built deeply into the GDRs burden-sharing system, and this for the very pragmatic reason that they specify a viable and defensible foundation for a true emergency program. Indeed, the GDRs burden-sharing system is *progressive with respect to both responsibility and capacity,* in that it defines both with respect to the development threshold.

We suggest here a development threshold set at $9,000/year (PPP).* This figure, while certainly subject to discussion, is a reasonable reflection of a level at which one has largely overcome the struggle against privation and become a bona fide member of the global consuming class. (And it is much more relevant to the problems here than the oft-cited figures of $1/day or $2/day for a global "poverty line.") It is above the global average income (of about $8,500), and might reasonably be called a "global middle class" income level (not to be confused with the significantly higher rich-world middle-class standard.) In terms of the trade-off that we actually face – at what point should poorer people help bear the burden, so that wealthier people would bear less? – it draws the line in just about the right place.

We define capacity as income, excluding all income below the development threshold. We similarly define responsibility as cumulative carbon emissions, excluding all emissions deriving from consumption below the development threshold. The logic here is that any burden-sharing framework designed to protect the right to development must necessarily exclude such "survival income" and "survival emissions." Also, it is important to note that capacity and responsibility are defined in individual terms, in a manner that takes explicit account of the distribution of income and emissions – inequality – within countries. This is critical. Relying merely on national per capita averages would fail to capture either the true depth of the development need or the actual extent of the national wealth.

Below, we estimate capacity and responsibility for all countries. (See Section 4.) We then combine those estimates (into a national "Responsibility and Capacity Indicator" – RCI) to quantify national mitigation and adaptation obligations corresponding to a

* See Appendix C for sensitivity analyses considering other thresholds.

	Percentage share of					
	Global population	Global income	Global capacity	Cumulative emissions 1990–2005	Global responsibility	Global RCI
United States	4.7	20.2	31.8	23.7	37.0	34.3
EU (27)	7.7	21.5	29.0	17.8	23.1	26.6
United Kingdom	0.9	3.3	4.7	2.5	3.6	4.3
Germany	1.3	4.0	5.6	3.8	5.2	5.5
Russia	2.2	2.5	1.5	7.4	4.3	2.3
Brazil	2.9	2.6	2.1	1.3	1.0	1.6
China	20.4	14.7	7.1	13.8	6.6	7.0
India	17.0	6.1	0.4	3.8	0.3	0.3
South Africa	0.7	0.9	0.8	1.6	1.5	1.1
LDCs	8.3	1.4	0.1	0.4	0.0	0.0
All high income	15.6	53.9	78.8	52.7	76.9	78.5
All middle income	47.7	36.6	20.7	41.1	22.8	21.1
All low income	36.7	9.5	0.5	6.2	0.4	0.5

Table ES-1. Global percentage shares of population, income, capacity, cumulative emissions, responsibility and RCI for selected countries and groups of countries.

global emergency program. The allocation of the burden along these lines * would see the United States bearing slightly more than one-third of the global burden, and the EU bearing roughly one quarter, whereas China bears less than one-fifteenth, and India less than one three-hundredth. (See Table ES 1 below.)

If, for example, it turns out that the total costs of the emergency program are 1 percent of gross world product, then the implied annual obligations average $780 for the people above the development threshold in the United States, and, similarly, $372 in the EU, $142 in China and $51 in India. (If the total costs turn out to be three percent of GWP, then triple these figures.)

Our conclusion is that if costs are shared within a progressive framework based on capacity and responsibility, then they will be shared in a manner that is both fair and fairly painless. We stress that, the higher these costs turn out to be, the *more* important it is to share them equitably, and note that, thankfully, the situation is not (yet) so dire that we are forced to consider truly heavy burdens and genuinely draconian decisions. Which is to say that it is still possible to avert climate catastrophe while pursuing sustainable human development, in good faith and on a global scale. Our world is a rich one in which, despite the climate crisis and even the broader environmental crisis, viable options remain.

The bad news is "merely" political, and amounts to two tasks. First, we must build the political will necessary to allocate a significant fraction of the gross world product (GWP) – 1 percent or perhaps even 3 – to implement a true emergency program. Second, we must ensure that the burden of that program is shared more or less along the lines of the "progressive global carbon tax" presented here. Both of these tasks are, admittedly, daunting, but it is time to recognize them for what they are – the necessary foundations of a viable global climate regime. Only if the relatively wealthy and relatively responsible (in both wealthier and poorer countries) pay the incremental costs of adaptation and clean-energy leapfrogging will those who need to prioritize development be able to do so.

* This could in theory be done via a global cap-and-allocate system. (See Section 5.)

In a world as bitterly divided as ours, a viable climate regime must at least do no harm, and this means that it must not erect further barriers to the progress of the poor. The key virtue of the Greenhouse Development Rights approach is that it does not do so. Indeed, it is because it does not do so that we can claim that the GDRs approach is in fact realistic. If the cost of meeting this condition is that, in the end, both mitigation and adaptation must be financed via a (fairly modest) tax on the luxury consumption of the relatively wealthy – for this is, finally, what GDRs proposes – well, what is this but realism about our actual conditions of life on this shared, finite planet?

Rosa Choque, who teaches other women how to boost their crops with compost, in Norte Potosi, south-west Bolivia. Farmers in the area say that the rainy season has halved in length and that torrential rains wash away their soil.

1 Introduction to the GDRs framework

The climate crisis is upon us. Indeed, it is long past time for an emergency program designed to stabilize the global climate and minimize the now inevitable destruction. Most all of us know this, yet despite our knowledge, the pace of our response has been profoundly inadequate. Nor is this slow pace entirely attributable to the intransigence of the current US Administration and its allies. There are deeper problems as well, and it is time now for them to take center stage. This paper thus begins with some clear assertions about the climate challenge, and the global climate policy impasse that must be broken if we are to face it successfully. We believe that all of these assertions are true. If so, they are also quite inconvenient.

First, the science now tells us that we are pushing beyond "*dangerous* anthropogenic interference with the climate system," and are on the verge of committing to *catastrophic* interference. Yet, even the more aggressive of today's "realist" scenarios (which seek to stabilize atmospheric greenhouse-gas concentrations at about 450 ppm CO_2-equivalent) accept a sharp likelihood that we will soon lock in the melting of the Greenland ice sheet, and with it a seven meter rise in the sea level.[1] In fact, if we want a good chance of preventing this melting, and a *decent likelihood* of staying below the widely endorsed 2°C threshold (and this would hardly mean that we were "safe"), then global emissions must peak very soon, and concentrations must be brought back to 400 ppm CO_2-equivalent or below. The best remaining path to such a goal requires that emissions peak within ten years – the sooner the better – and then decline precipitously.[2] As implausible as this may seem, it is the trajectory that the climate science is forcing us to accept, if we actually want a reasonable likelihood of keeping below 2°C. To achieve such a trajectory, however, we will have to be far more aggressive than even the most ambitious of the current EU and US proposals.[3]

Second, we confront the climate crisis, and the consequent need for an emergency program, in a profoundly divided world characterized by both staggering levels of poverty and enormous (and growing) wealth. This is a world in which the usual path from poverty to prosperity is via a development process that entails dramatic increases in the per capita use of fossil fuel energy and other non-renewable resources. And this path, alas, must be closed. Indeed, any future in which it is taken by even a significant fraction of the world's poor is a future in which dramatically rising carbon emissions make a mockery of emergency rhetoric. Nor will finding our way to an alternative be easy. Yet, if we are to have any chance at all – if any emergency program is to have any hope of being embraced – we must take care that it does not threaten to lock in today's vast disparities of wealth and income. Rather, it must show that it can drive down emissions, globally, even while ambitious development goals are met and surpassed.[4] To this end, it must slash the emissions of the already wealthy and, at the same time, prevent the unbounded emissions growth of those rising out of poverty. *And it must do so without stifling their development aspirations.*

It is a tall order, and it leads us, inevitably, to the intersection of the climate crisis and the development crisis, and to the core of the climate challenge: The world's wealthy minority has left precious little space for the poor majority. So little space that, even if industrialized country emissions were suddenly and magically halted, the dramatic emissions reduction demanded by the climate crisis would still require the developing countries to urgently decarbonize their economies, and to do so while they were still combating endemic poverty. This conclusion – a direct consequence of the implacable mathematics of our vanishing emissions budget – is not only the core of the physical challenge, but also the crux of the international political impasse that has overtaken the negotiations.

As long as there is no acceptable burden-sharing proposal on the table, one that ensures that an emergency program can be executed without stifling development in the South, developing-country negotiators can be forgiven if they conclude that their countries have more to lose than to gain from earnest engagement. This is especially true because an emergency program would not be free. We might be smart, and lucky, and rapid mitigation might actually be cheap. It might even provide so much economic stimulus that overall costs would be negative.[5] But, frankly, such outcomes do not strike us as being particularly likely. It is not simply that so much time has been wasted; it is that each day we waste more, and that we may not be lucky at all. Given this, and given particularly the social, sectoral and political dynamics that would attend any true emergency mitigation program, its costs may in the end be quite large. And to them must be added the costs of adaptation, as essential as mitigation in any emergency program and quite possibly even more costly.

Conventional wisdom, alas, tells us that the world's wealthier citizens cannot be expected to pay more than a trivial amount for climate change, and even less if the payments go to people and projects in "other countries." In fact, given today's extremely limited "willingness to pay," the costs of a true emergency program may be politically unsupportable even if the overall costs of mitigation turn out to be quite low, and even if we yield to the (great) temptation to put adaptation aside. Thus, southern negotiators may be forgiven if they fear that a stringent global climate agreement would saddle them with unacceptable costs and permanently constrain their development. Recent history, after all, is one in which high-sounding schemes, celebrated in the halls of global power, seldom resolve, in the villages and megacities, into just and adequate results. Given this, the reticence of southern negotiators has been a useful habit, and even a wise one. In any case, poor countries, if they see mitigation as unfairly competing with development and poverty alleviation, will balk at it. Which is why, before finally throwing their support behind an emergency program, southern negotiators will need to see a proposal that, above all else, explicitly safeguards the right to development.

Nor will an "equal per capita emissions right" serve as an acceptable substitute for such a right. This is a long story, but it comes, in the end, to a simple fact: Given that the global carbon budget is already largely depleted, it is too late for *emissions rights* of any kind to protect *developmental equity*. Which is why, though per-capita allocation has traditionally been resisted by the North, it will prove even less acceptable to the South.[6] Ultimately, the international climate policy impasse demands strategies that reconcile the twin challenges of climate and development directly, without trying to offer equal emissions rights as a proxy. It demands a climate regime that acknowledges the right to development, and then places that right at its structural core. The bottom line is that such a regime must secure for the developing nations a viable portion of the scant remaining atmospheric space, and do so in a manner that allows them to prosper within it.

To be specific, the GDRs framework embodies the right to development as a "development threshold" below which individuals, by definition poor, are not expected to share the burden of mitigating the climate problem. This threshold reflects a level of welfare beyond basic needs, but well short of today's levels of "affluent" consumption. People below it have little responsibility for the climate problem and relatively little capacity to invest in solving it. Indeed, they have development as their proper priority, and cannot be saddled with the costs of keeping society as a whole within the starkly limited global carbon budget.

People above the development threshold, who have arguably realized their right to development, face the corresponding responsibility to preserve that right for others. It is they who must share the burden – in accordance with the UNFCCC's broad principle of "common but differentiated responsibility and respective capabilities" – of funding the emergency program.[7] It is they who must bear the costs of not only curbing the emissions associated with their own consumption, but also of ensuring that, as those below the threshold rise toward and then above it, they are able to do so along sustainable, low-emission paths.

In practice, of course, obligations and commitments within a climate regime would have to be aggregated and allocated on a national level. But it still makes sense, and is more transparent and justifiable, to define and quantify these commitments in terms that recognize today's stark intranational differences in responsibility and capacity. Which is why the GDRs framework highlights the indisputable fact that it is people – and not nations or economies – that possess the right to development. And that this, inescapably, means taking inequality *within* countries as seriously as inequality *between* countries. To be sure, this focus on intranational inequity will be one of the most controversial aspect of the GDRs framework, but it is also, we believe, the key to breaking the climate impasse.

In all this, "responsibility" and "capacity" are not mere pretty words, featured here because they are prominently embodied in the Framework Convention. Rather, they are built deeply into the GDRs burden-sharing system, and this for the very pragmatic reason that they specify a viable and defensible foundation for a true emergency program. There is a lot to say about this – from the limits of per capita approaches to the need for a principle-based framework to the necessity of a system that can support adaptation as well as mitigation – but ultimately, this is largely a pragmatic matter. The resources for an emergency program have to come from somewhere, and it is the world's wealthy who have the necessary "ways and means." That is the capacity side of the equation. As for responsibility, we may soon find, with the brunt of the impacts falling on poor and innocent people around the world, that it counts a great deal, not only morally but politically as well. As matters worsen, the rich and the responsible will not be able to stand safely aloof.

In the discussion below, we show calculations illustrating the implications of a consistent responsibility and capacity-based approach that is designed to safeguard the right to development. In particular, we calculate a national Responsibility and Capacity Indicator (RCI) that takes explicit account of the distribution of income and emissions – inequality – within countries. We then use this RCI to quantify national mitigation and adaptation obligations corresponding to an emergency program. And we demonstrate a critical, even decisive fact: Even if its costs were fairly large, the world's wealthier citizens could easily bear an emergency global climate stabilization program; it would not impoverish them. In fact, they could do so with relatively modest reductions in their luxury consumption.

1.1 A reference framework

We, of course, realize that approaches like this are outside the spectrum of proposals now being considered for a post-2012 regime. But at the same time, it is plainly true that the negotiations could use a bit of honesty and boldness. In this context, we believe that the GDRs framework can serve as a useful standard of comparison – a "reference framework" that clearly marks out a set of essential core elements, which must be part of any even potentially successful climate regime.

The GDRs framework, particularly, aims to highlight the deep structure of the climate problem, and by so doing to illuminate the structure of the necessary solution. It refuses to prejudge solutions based on today's passing standards of political acceptability. Against such a reference, more "realistic" regime proposals can be measured to determine how realistic they actually are, from the only standpoint that really matters: enabling equitable, sustainable development, while having a real chance of preventing climate catastrophe.

Flooding is a major problem for the people of El Molino Sur in Matagalpa, central Nicaragua. Here they are building up the local river bank, to protect their homes during the wet season.

2 The urgency

It is not our task to justify the 2°C threshold. There is little doubt that even before the temperature increase reaches that level, our ability to meet critical objectives – food and water security in poor countries, for example, or the preservation of ecological diversity – will be severely challenged. And while adaptation can help, and indeed will be an absolute necessity if we are to avoid the worst effects of even the most immediate impacts, it is not sufficient. Indeed, the IPCC's recent Fourth Assessment Report of Working Group II makes clear that increasingly severe consequences are largely inevitable, given the warming that is already "in the pipeline."

So it is with some reluctance that we admit that, even with our rather expansive view of what is possible in terms of mitigation, humanity has already lost the ability to stay with certainty below the 2°C threshold. Nevertheless, we must try our best. If we do not, 2°C of warming will become inevitable, and catastrophic impacts all but inevitable. Figure 1 is designed to illustrate this situation. It shows three progressively ambitious global emission reduction trajectories, the weakest of which is just barely stringent enough to be called an emergency trajectory.[8] And, following the current understanding of the relevant scientific uncertainties, it shows estimated probabilities that each trajectory would actually overshoot the 2°C line.[9]

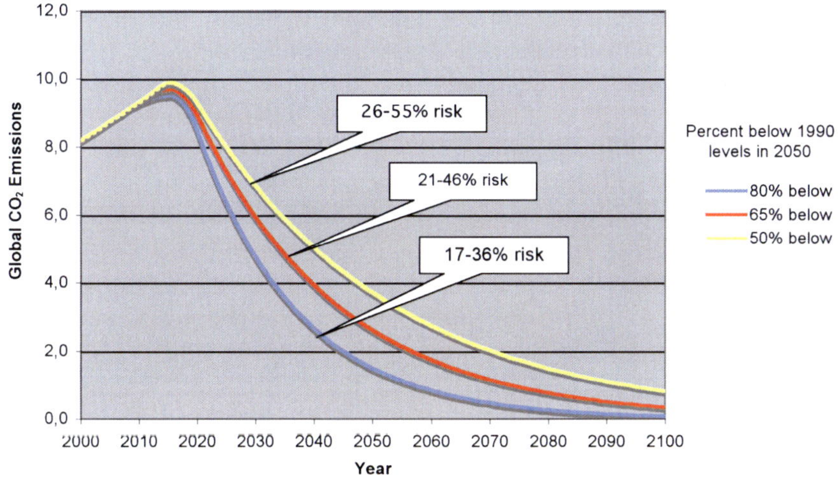

Figure 1. Emissions pathways for three emergency scenarios, peaking in 2015, and falling to roughly 50%, 65%, and 80% below 1990 levels in 2050, along with each scenario's estimated risk of exceeding the 2°C threshold.

The most stringent of these trajectories is, as you can easily see, heroic indeed. It has emissions peaking in 2015 and dropping off at a resolute 6 percent per year, reaching a level of 80 percent below 1990 levels in 2050. Along the way, CO_2 concentrations peak at about 425 ppm (with CO_2-equivalent levels[10] reaching about 470 ppm) before they begin to fall. Yet, even with this effort, almost inconceivable[11] in today's political environment, we would still be exposed to an alarming 17–36 percent risk of exceeding 2°C.

The least radical of these trajectories also peaks in 2015, though at a somewhat higher level, and reaches 50 percent below 1990 levels in 2050 with reductions at about 3.4 percent annually after 2020. Carbon dioxide concentrations peak at about 445 ppm-CO_2 (with CO_2-equivalent levels reaching about 500 ppm), leaving us with a roughly 26–55 percent risk of exceeding 2°C before 2100.

This least radical trajectory represents an important benchmark in the current debate, for it marks the border between trajectories that scientists can accept as being plausibly precautionary and trajectories that "realists" consider economically plausible. NASA scientist James Hansen, for example, warns that "We have to stabilize emissions of carbon dioxide within a decade" or the temperature "will be warmer than it has been for half a million years, and many things could become unstoppable."[12] Thus, unsurprisingly, this least radical trajectory is only barely consistent with the highest acceptable targets suggested by the Climate Action Network International in a recent submission to the UN process,[13] and with the similarly daunting conclusions of the Scientific Expert Group convened by Sigma Xi for the United Nations Foundation.[14] Yet, at the same time, it is roughly the lowest target deemed economically feasible by the Stern Review.[15]

All things considered, these three trajectories mark a critical band, the one that, if we are serious, we have to aim for. Consider them to define the "honest emergency trajectories," and note that, as such, they essentially span the lowest category of modeled scenarios reported in the IPCC's 2007 assessment.[16]

We willingly admit that a 2015 global emissions peak will be seen by many as unrealistic, and that even some climate activists will judge it unwise or unhelpful to alarm people with such low emissions scenarios. The point, however, is to inject some honesty into the debate. *Too often, earnest calls to avoid "dangerous climate change" by keeping the warming below 2°C are accompanied by apparently sanguine recommendations for emissions pathways or reduction targets that have virtually no chance of meeting that goal.* Frankly, the Stern Review's litany of climate impacts can almost certainly *not* be prevented by stabilizing greenhouse gas concentrations within most of its own recommended range of 450–550 ppm CO_2-equivalent. And though most G8 governments are, at least officially, committed to meeting the 2°C target, it will almost certainly *not* be attained by the global reduction target (50 percent reductions by 2050) recommended in 2007's G8 declaration. These may be inconvenient truths; they may indeed be obvious ones, but they are truths nonetheless, and bracing ones. And given how soon and quickly emissions need to drop, there is no real alternative to clearly repeating them. Certainly the ecosystems – and many of the people – that are most at risk are unable to do so for themselves. If they could, they would no doubt find even our most stringent scenario to be unacceptably dangerous.

For these reasons, we will use the lowest of these pathways – which we will refer to as the "2°C emergency pathway" – as our reference. This makes sense because, of the three trajectories, it has the lowest risk of exceeding 2°C, and because the necessary social and technological transformations will be no less profound in the two less stringent cases. It is, in other words, our proper marker trajectory, the one that best stands for "an honest reckoning" and thus the one most appropriate to our purposes. Besides, our results do not change significantly unless we relax to a trajectory that is far weaker, and far more dangerous, than even the least radical of our plausible emergency pathways.

Emergency action demands heroic efforts. And such efforts are justified because we still have a chance of holding the 2°C line. Already existing technologies – if implemented and disseminated with Manhattan Project urgency – can very quickly win us huge emissions reductions, and buy us time to develop newer technologies and adopt lower-impact lifestyles. But we cannot afford any more delays, not even those associated with "realism," which seems today to demand that each small increment of progress be made to appear economically unthreatening and politically "win-win." The truth is that, given the speed at which we now have to move, there are going to be costs, and losers, and it is time to admit it. And plan for it. Costs, after all, can be fairly shared, and losers can be supported and compensated.

In short, we need an emergency program, and the costs of such a program, while affordable, are likely to be considerably greater than is our current willingness to pay. In the next section, we will explore the background conditions – in particular, the divisions between the wealthy and the poor that undergird both the development crisis and the climate crisis – that will have to be taken into proper account if we are going to seriously try to break the climate impasse.

Coastal communities in south-west Bangladesh have seen their fresh water turned salty by the rising sea. So they have turned skywards, some using traditional rainwater harvesting clay pots such as this one. Pots are placed underneath corrugated iron roofing, to catch the rainwater which runs off. Gauze and a lid at the top help to exclude mosquitos and other harmful organisms, and both the roof and pot are regularly cleaned with bleach.

3 Human development and climate protection

Even as we grow anxious and even terrified by a sense of impending climate catastrophe, many of the world's people are necessarily preoccupied with another, even more pressing crisis: that of poverty. Much can be and has been said about this crisis – scandalously high infant mortality rates, horrific though easily preventable disease as a miserable fact of life and death, physical insecurity, denial of opportunity and the right to a productive, fulfilling and dignified life; all in a world of extreme affluence and growing middle-class wealth. We shall not attempt to repeat it all here.

But there are things that must be said about poverty – and therefore inequality and wealth – and the climate crisis. First, there is no road to development, however conceived, that does not greatly improve access to energy services. Yet, as economies are now structured, as development is now envisioned, and as long as we rely on today's energy technologies, this will imply increases in CO_2 emissions that are entirely incompatible with a precautionary climate policy. And thus our dilemma: There is simply not enough "environmental space" for the still-poor to develop in the same way – or in anything like the same way – as that which was taken by the already-rich.

It is no mystery where this environmental space has gone. The 15 percent of the world's population that lives today in the roughly 40 high-income countries uses about half the world's energy, produces about half the world's CO_2 and consumes about half the world's goods and services. Further, the world's wealthy, as they developed into this current resource-intensive state, consumed so great a fraction of the carbon budget that, today, we are faced with the grim task of allocating an entirely inadequate remainder.

And thus our current dilemma: If we are to keep within the scant remaining budget, global emissions must quickly peak and then precipitously decline. Yet, with today's business-as-usual technologies, if the poor majority's energy consumption reaches even half the per capita level of the wealthy minority, then global CO_2 emissions would essentially double. And herein lies the essential tension between the aspirations of the world's poor – and even the minimal demands of basic human development – and, on the other side, the climate challenge. Any climate regime that ignores it is doomed to failure.

Figure 2 expresses this tension graphically by way of a comparison of emissions trajectories. The three "peak and decline" trajectories are the same as those shown above in Figure 1, but here we compare them to the "South's B1 pathway," which is a rather optimistic reference projection of the South's future emissions (derived from the IPCC's "sustainable" B1 scenario).[17] The result is a simple but unambiguous demonstration of the radical inconsistency between a truly precautionary trajectory and even this relatively green reference projection, one that shows that, if we are to avoid bursting through the range of plausibly precautionary global pathways, the South's emissions must leave their projected path almost immediately, and be dropping precipitously by 2025.[18] And even with the B1 storyline's optimistic assumptions about both equity and economic growth, many people in the South would still be struggling against poverty when its emissions had to begin this steep decline.[19] Moreover, the less stringent pathways – despite their substantially higher risks of catastrophic climate change – provide only another few extra years of emissions growth. All of which highlights the central question: What manner of climate regime can enable such a rapid emissions decline while at the same time enabling the nations of the South to not only continue, but even step up, their fight against poverty?

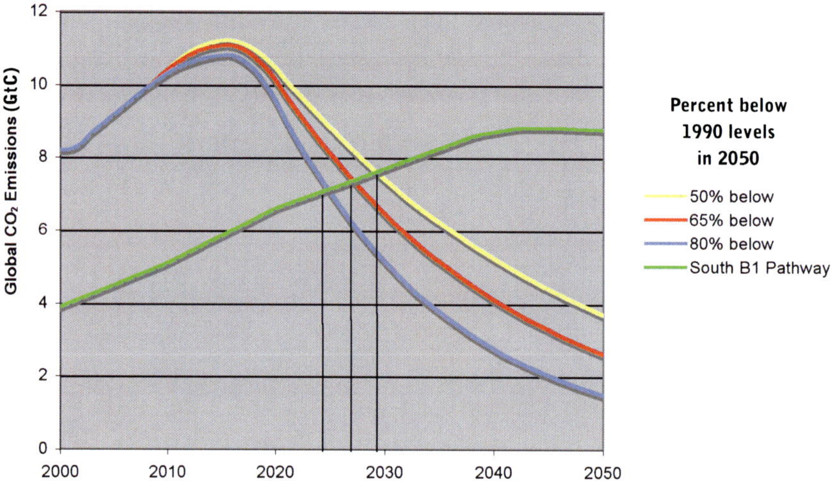

Figure 2. Available global emissions budget under three increasingly stringent reduction scenarios. All peak in 2015, and fall, respectively, to 50%, 65%, and 80% below 1990 levels by 2050. (See Section 2). All are plotted along with southern emissions (according to the IPCC's B1 scenario).

Here then is the crux of the climate-development dilemma: Under a global emergency pathway, carbon constraints would be so tight that, in the absence of explicit efforts to enable low-emissions development, the poor would be badly squeezed. In effect, they would lose their right to development. More precisely, the emergency pathway would be seen as requiring development to be deferred, so that limited resources could be invested instead in mitigation, and in consequence it would be resisted. Nor would this resistance be mere intransigence or brinksmanship. It would, in many cases, be a rational accounting of necessity.

3.1 The right to development

If we are to successfully pursue an emergency climate stabilization program, our agenda must expand beyond climate stabilization. A global climate regime with any promise of success must also *embrace the right to sustainable human development, and it must do so explicitly*. This right must be declared and pursued, despite even the dire pressures of the climate crisis. Any emergency program that does not do so will flounder and fail.

We do not mean that development must put economic growth above the protection of the climate. Just the opposite. We are referring specifically to *human develop-*

ment, a difficult notion that we may perhaps define as the satisfaction of fundamental needs in a manner that frees people from the vulnerability and deprivation of poverty and makes possible a decent level of security and well-being. The challenge lies in ensuring the right to such development in a manner that properly links it with an emergency drive to rapidly decarbonize the entire global economy.

Incidentally, we are lucky that it is still possible to pursue sustainable human development, in good faith and on a global scale. The situation is not (yet) so dire or the scale of the needed response so overwhelming that we are forced to make genuinely draconian decisions. We are lucky that our world is a rich and resourceful one in which, despite the climate crisis and even the larger environmental crisis, viable options remain. We need only find a way to embrace those options, and if this means allocating a significant fraction of the gross world product (GWP) – 1 percent or even 3 – to enabling the low-carbon transition, then what of it? We can afford it. It is not actually a lot of money. Not compared to the alternative.

This was Nicholas Stern's point,[20] and it bears repeating. And it is just the beginning of the tale. For there is no economic law that tells us that, having made the transition to a low-carbon path, we would not find it to be at least as economically convivial as this one. There is no economic law that precludes rational public policies, or that demands that destructive subsidies continue, or that insists that economic statistics continue to be warped and deformed by a nonsensical blindness to human and natural well-being. There is no law, indeed, that mandates that even wealthy countries, having committed themselves to a climate transition that made real demands, would not subsequently discover that they benefited enormously from it, and this even if it meant a small slowing in the rate of conventionally measured economic growth.

The point here, the one that must not be lost, is that we waste far more in building, adapting to, and maintaining ill-conceived infrastructure than we would need to not only decarbonize the entire global economy, but to do so in a manner that simultaneously meets all basic human needs. Having stipulated this, we can return to our central claim, that any effective climate regime must preserve the right to sustainable human development.

There are two aspects to this claim. First, there is the political imperative to embrace human development. For even as we seek a path to an emergency climate response, southern negotiators will insist – with strong ethical and political justification – that their priority must be lifting up their poor, not mitigating greenhouse gas emissions. They will assert this, moreover, despite strong and accumulating evidence that even globally non-catastrophic climate changes will still cause immense local damages, undermining many of the development gains that poor communities have thus far managed to achieve. Not that this evidence is much at issue, or that southern negotiators deny it, but they nevertheless do not make mitigation a first tier priority. Perhaps they cannot, not while their development needs are so great and pressing, and certainly not while northern policies – climate policies but also trade policies, and intellectual-rights policies, and development policies in general – remain equivocal or even counter-productive.

Some matters are clear. One is that the people of the developing world are unlikely to *prioritize* low-carbon development, not if it means paying a premium for energy services while so many among them have not even achieved basic levels of, say, food security. Another is that southern negotiators will remain focused on macroeconomic growth as a route to poverty reduction for the many (as well as, of course, riches for the few) and that any climate regime that even appears to threaten such growth will be an extremely tough sell. This, moreover, will probably remain the case even as the impacts of climate change worsen and become more obvious, for even then the opportunity costs of mitigation expenditures, which could otherwise be spent on social welfare programs, will be an issue.

Even more importantly, there is a structural imperative to engage the problem of human development. Simply put, there are so many intrinsic connections between the climate and human development challenges that, as a practical matter, we can only hope to successfully engage the climate problem if the poor majority is visibly progressing toward genuine human development. These connections, though manifold and complex, can be briefly outlined with respect to both mitigation and adaptation. In the former case, an emergency program would require dramatic technological transformation, amounting to a wholesale reinvention of the global energy infrastructure on the basis of low-emission technologies. In the South, this reinvention would require large-scale investment in training and education, as well as creating the institutional capacity to adopt, develop and implement revolutionary solutions, all while simultaneously meeting the growing needs of expanding populations and economies. An emergency program would also require far-reaching changes in agricultural and land-use practices, which currently account for as much as one-third of southern greenhouse-gas emissions. These changes are possible, but only if there is a real commitment to the grassroots empowerment that is essential if any truly positive future is to open to the poor communities that are now dependent on land-clearing for subsistence farming, fuel-wood harvesting, grazing and timber extraction.[21] The point is that this dependence must be broken, but this cannot happen without a new focus on, and new investment in, human development. Indeed, such investment is fundamental to any rapid transition, which depends not only on next-generation energy technologies, but also on female literacy, not only on new agronomic technologies, but also on universal neonatal healthcare.

As far as adaptation is concerned, the importance of human development is even clearer. Adaptation to climate change clearly requires a level of "resilience" that is far beyond the grasp of the billions of people that are still mired in poverty. And we know this despite being unable to anticipate the precise impacts that climate change will impose on the poor, let alone describe the exact mechanisms that will be necessary to counter-balance the harm that they will suffer from climate destabilization. After all, poor households and communities endure a range of stresses, many of which are being exacerbated by climate change, and together they create a syndrome of vulnerability. Thus, adaptation calls for investments that create options and reserves. It requires improved access to finance and technology, but just as importantly it demands social capital and enfranchisement. In other words, it takes more than narrow, climate-focused measures to "build adaptive capacity." Which is to say that, while it might help to provide an agricultural household a more drought-resistant variety of a staple crop, it will not by itself enable them to weather the next drought. Such a family will have far better odds if there is a literate family member, if they can access investment capital through local financial institutions, if they enjoy relatively intact social networks, if they can hold policymakers accountable. As Amartya Sen famously said, famines do not happen in democracies.

But here is a proviso. Though these arguments echo a deep sense of ethical propriety, the Greenhouse Development Rights approach is not fundamentally an appeal to morality. Its real justification is a realist one. The GDRs framework, or something like it, will be necessary if we are to break the global impasse and rise to the demands of the climate crisis, and this for two simple reasons: *The North cannot stabilize the climate without the full commitment of the South, and the South cannot make that commitment if doing so would threaten to undermine its development.* In practice, this means that a global alliance to stabilize the climate can only arise, and survive, on terms that honor the poor world's right to development. The wealthy countries must not only cut their own emissions, deeply and soon, but also do whatever is necessary to help the poor leapfrog into a low-emissions, high-adaptation future.

3.2 A development threshold

Greenhouse Development Rights suggests a framework for such an alliance, by way of this simple but critical bit of clarification: In our environmentally constrained world, the right to development is not a right to economic growth as such, but rather the right to a modest but dignified level of well-being. We define this level by way of a *development threshold*. Below this threshold, individuals must be allowed to prioritize development. This means that they should not have to help bear the burdens of dealing with the changing climate, on either the mitigation or the adaptation sides. Those above the threshold, on the other hand, must help to shoulder these burdens, and this regardless of whether they happen to live in the North or in the South. It is they, after all, who have the capacity to do so, as it is they who bear the overwhelming share of the responsibility for the threatened climate.

The level at which such a development threshold would best be set is a matter for debate, but the relevant principles are clear, as is the goal. The development threshold should differentiate the global poor, who have pressing and legitimate unmet needs, from the "global middle class," which has reached a level of consumption that yields an appreciable contribution to the climate problem, and has similarly acquired enough capacity to help bear the costs of managing that problem, however high or low they ultimately turn out to be.

Defining the development threshold in a concrete and quantitative sense is, not surprisingly, tricky. The most straightforward option is to define it in terms of income level, though this option suffers a number of obvious problems. Income, after all, is a simplistic and one-dimensional indicator that quite inaccurately reflects sustainable human development. It prioritizes a certain mode of development – economic growth – while obscuring the importance of human rights, political enfranchisement, liberty, social capital, health, environmental and physical security, all of which are essential to a decent standard of human well-being. Nevertheless, we will stick for now with this purely economic indicator, for three principal reasons. First, income is highly correlated with important indicators of well-being, and this particularly at the income levels that span the low- and middle-income countries, where there is an indisputable linkage between income and basic indicators such as infant mortality, life expectancy, malnourishment and educational attainment. Second, income does indeed reflect the capacity to pay for mitigation and adaptation, especially once a country is wealthy enough for basic needs to be met. Third, income is a helpful proxy for consumption, and hence for the distribution of carbon emissions within a country, and hence for responsibility.

How then, should we set the development threshold? Our claim is that a "dignified level of human development free from the privations of poverty" implies a line higher than a "poverty line," that it indeed implies something like 150 percent of a poverty-line income. This particular level is, of course, somewhat arbitrary, but its appropriateness is supported by the many other contexts in which such a level is taken to define the upper boundary of "exempt" or "lifeline" income. These include starting points for income tax calculations, eligibility thresholds for social services, and criteria for defining "economically vulnerable" or "near-poor" populations. Thus, while it might be an underestimate, we will take it as a plausible and indicative figure, and as a good starting point for discussion. In any event, the principle it is meant to illustrate is clear, and the latitude for meaningful negotiation is not extremely broad.

So, what is a sensible "global poverty line?" If anything is certain, it is that it is not the typical figures of $1 per day or $2 per day.[22] Indeed, such low figures obscure the real meaning of poverty, and the real nature of the poverty crisis. The $1 a day line, more precisely, is a *"destitution line,"* and the $2 a day line an *"extreme poverty line."* Moreover, this is obvious. A person's income can grow much higher that $2 a day and they still face pervasive exposure to the plagues of poverty: malnutrition, high infant mortality, low educational attainment, high relative food expenditures. A defensible global poverty line, on the other hand, must reflect the income level at which these plagues begin to disappear, or at least become exceptions to the rule. It must, certainly, exceed the point at which the Millennium Development Goals have been largely met. All of which is to raise empirical and statistical questions that we will not dwell on here. In any case, as it unsurprisingly turns out, the evidence suggests that a global poverty line should be defined to be well above the extreme poverty line. It is more like $16 a day, or, equivalently, $6,000 a year.[23] (Note, since this $6,000 figure is in PPP terms, it converts to a lower income level in a local developing country currency than if it were converted at market exchange rates.)

Taking $6,000 a year as the global poverty line, we then have an indicative development threshold of $9,000 a year. This is well above the global median income (of about $3,500 in 2005), and just slightly above the global average income (of about $8,500). It might reasonably be called a "global middle class" income level (not to be confused with the significantly higher rich-world middle-class standard). And we think that, in terms of the trade-off we actually face – *at what point should poorer people help bear the burden, so that wealthier people would bear less?* – it draws the line in just about the right place.

This is not to say that poverty and hardship do not persist above an income level of $9,000 a year. Nor is it to say that a higher development threshold could not be strongly defended. But for the purposes of clarifying the principles that the development threshold is meant to embody, and thus enabling us to illustrate the implications of the GDRs framework for national climate obligations, we will take $9,000 a year as our indicative development threshold, as we will take those people whose incomes are above it, be they middle-class or wealthy, to be members of the global consuming class. (Note that the appendix contain a sensitivity analysis that demonstrates the implications of higher and lower figures.)

Crucially, we reckon the development threshold as an *individual*, not *national* average, threshold. Countries with per capita incomes below $9,000 a year always have subpopulations with higher incomes, and smaller subpopulations with *far* higher incomes, and vice versa. The more unequal a country, the more this is the case. Thus, we stress that it should be poor individuals, not poor nations, who are excused from bearing climate-related obligations. Individuals with incomes above the development threshold – even if they live in countries with average incomes below the threshold – should be accountable for their fair share of the global climate burden. Similarly, national obligations should be reckoned in accordance with the obligations of their individual inhabitants. This, in a world of nations, is the only reasonable approach to the problem here.

This proposition – that the consuming class in developing countries has no greater claim on the remaining environmental space than do its peers in wealthy countries – will of course be controversial. Taken seriously, it necessarily challenges the conventional wisdom that there is a unified "South," composed in meaningful degree by nations and peoples with overwhelmingly common interests. Nevertheless, the realities here can no longer be denied, as was illustrated in "Worlds collide in India over global warming," an article that appeared in the *Financial Times* during 2007's G8+5 meeting.[24] Its central point – indeed its central warning – was that Mukesh Ambani, the world's 14th richest man, is now busily building himself a 60-storey glass palace in Mumbai. The key statistic is that this "home," which sports a helipad, a pool, parking for 168 luxury cars and quarters for an army of staff, is estimated to cost half a billion US dollars. The key quote: "Such self-indulgence should be a reminder that the G8 is dealing with not one India when it comes to climate change, but two: first-world India and third-world India."

To be sure, Bill Gates[25] is three times richer than Mukesh Ambani. But the point is still clear. The developing world, despite its millions of desperately poor people, contains a substantial and growing class of people that are reveling in northern-style consumption – some of it quite absurd in its conspicuousness. Just as obviously, this wealthy class has both a non-negligible degree of responsibility for the climate problem and the capacity to help solve it.

More particularly, intranational inequality must be taken into explicit account if we want to meaningfully calculate, and compare, the capacities of wealthy countries such as the United States with those of emerging but still developing countries such as China and India. Indeed, attempts to do so without properly considering inequality – without exempting the incomes and emissions of people below a development threshold, and counting those of people above it – are logically and politically absurd. As if the small incomes of impoverished peasants should be taken to increase Chinese or Indian capacity to mitigate emissions in a global energy regime they in no way benefit from. As if Mr. Ambani's billions, for their part, should be ignored.

Not that all cases are as clear cut. The "global middle class" holds a more ambiguous position than either Mukesh Ambani or Bill Gates, and the precise location of the development threshold may be quite fairly debated. But the main point is obvious. Recognizing inequality *within* countries is as unavoidable as recognizing inequality *between* countries. If, that is, our goal is a burden-sharing system that actually makes ethical and political sense. There is just no way around it. Any burden-sharing system that even implicitly asks poor- or middle-class people in wealthy countries to put their shoulders to the wheel, while at the same time exempting wealthy people in poor countries from the same effort does not have a chance. Nor, just as crucially, does any system that asks wealthy- and middle-class people in poor countries to bear a burden that is defined, by convenient fiction, as if their poor were part of the problem. They are not.

3.3 Burden sharing in the greenhouse

Fundamentally, the GDRs framework is a rich/poor burden-sharing arrangement designed to support an emergency program while protecting the right to development. It does so by allocating the costs of that program among those above the development threshold – irrespective of whether they live in wealthy or developing countries – while allowing those below that threshold to attend to their development priorities.

The keys here are the two notions that lie at the core of most burden-sharing discussions: capacity and responsibility. The idea that burden sharing should be based on a systematic treatment of responsibility and capacity is not new, and is reflected in most, if not all, contemporary proposals. These tend to be "multi-stage" proposals that, at a minimum, exempt poor countries from any quantified (or, more importantly, cost-bearing) obligations, and at a maximum divide countries into classes defined by measures of income and emissions.[26] Not only are these moves intuitively sensible, but they are consistent with the principle of "common but differentiated responsibilities and respective capabilities" enshrined in the UNFCCC itself.

3.3.1 Defining capacity

Capacity reflects wealth. For our purposes, it reflects the portion of national wealth that can reasonably be tapped to respond to the climate crisis. But all wealth is not equal. Its definition must be reconciled with the right to development, which is to say that capacity must be calculated, and the climate burden shared, in a manner that takes proper account of intranational inequality.

To see this, assume that the emergency program is to be funded through a global tax (and this, in a sense, is what a burden-sharing system amounts to) on each country's capacity. Now consider an overly simple example in which a country's capacity is defined as its total income (GDP). Thus, a country's share of the global mitigation and adaptation burdens would be exactly equal to its share of total global income. Straightforwardly, if the total "global bill" for the emergency program is 1 percent of the total global income (the GWP), this bill would be covered if each country paid 1 percent of its national income.

But this sort of "flat tax," when used within countries to raise domestic revenue, is almost uniformly rejected as unfair. The poor are generally seen as deserving lower tax rates because, the poorer you are, the more of your income you spend on "necessities", and the richer you are, the more of your income you spend on "luxuries." So if a dollar in taxes has to be taken from someone, it is fairer to take it from someone who will then have to reduce their luxury consumption than from someone who would have to reduce their consumption of necessities. *In other words, the consumption of the poor has a greater moral priority than the consumption of the rich.* For this reason, tax systems are generally progressive. They exempt from taxation income below some specified minimum threshold. Also, the tax rate on income above this threshold typically increases as income rises, increasing the progressivity of the overall system.

But the exemption alone is enough to ensure that such a distribution of the tax burden is basically progressive.

One simple way to approximate the same progressive effect in a global burden-sharing system would be to define national capacity as the amount by which a country's average per capita income exceeds some minimal threshold. This threshold could be set to equal the development threshold, as defined above, thus ensuring that the portion of a country's GDP that fell below the development threshold would be exempt from being "taxed" to pay for the global emergency program. And, after all, to the degree that a country's GDP lies below the development threshold, it is likely to be paying for necessities that contribute directly to subsistence and development, rather than for luxuries.

The logic here is akin to that of the southern negotiators who have, in the past, successfully argued that developing countries should be granted an exemption from any obligation to pay for climate mitigation. This argument, however, is fast losing its moral force, and for the entirely justifiably reason that it ignores the "North within the South" – a rising consuming class in the developing world that has more in common with its brethren in the North than with the poor majorities within its own countries. In other words, by focusing on average per capita income, this traditional argument obscures income disparities *within* countries, which are fully as significant as income disparities *between* countries.

What to do? Our approach is to define capacity in a manner that accounts for income disparities within countries. To define it, that is, as *individual income* in excess of the development threshold, summed across all the individuals in a country, from the poorest peasant to the wealthiest tycoon. Ultimately, since this is all toward the end of a global climate agreement between nations, capacity will be defined – and the climate burden allocated – on a national basis. But the point here is that, unless capacity is calculated in a manner that accounts for intranational inequality, it will not meaningfully reflect the development status – the wealth and poverty – of nations.

3.3.2 Defining responsibility

Responsibility, of course, is the central concept behind the "polluter pays" principle. And, like capacity, it has a strong common-sense resonance. The notion of national "responsibility for greenhouse gas pollution" is intuitively – and correctly – understood in terms of the greenhouse gases that nations have emitted. As such, the baseline definition of responsibility must be in terms of cumulative emissions, though there are obviously complications in defining and measuring it unambiguously.

Some of these are serious. There are, for example, the disjoint but overlapping responsibilities of people and nations. When a man moves from country A to country B, does his past responsibility travel with him? What if a country splits in two, or three? What if it is pillaged, or overtaken by another? Do a country's citizens have responsibility for the actions of its leaders? What, and this is a pertinent case, if a country suffers (or suffered) from illegitimate leadership and a lack of effective democracy?

Then there is the matter of time. From what point should historical emissions count toward a nation's responsibility? The potential risks of global warming were first identified by Svente Arrhenius in 1896, were included in some university curricula in the 1940s, and were recognized in studies by the Johnson Administration in the United States in the 1960s. It is commonplace to suggest that "responsibility" for greenhouse pollution should start in 1990, when the first report of the IPCC made the risks widely and publicly evident, but as even this capsule history makes plain, *some people*, including advisers to the president of the United States, have known about the risks for a much longer time.

The greatest of these problems, however, is that of intention. Initially, our nations had a *default* policy of inaction, one that arose from simple ignorance and was entirely excusable. Over time, however, this ignorance was attenuated. Dangers were mooted, but in general they were brushed aside and we shifted to a policy of *active* inaction, of denial disguised as "risk-management." This policy was, of course, based on short-term and sectoral interests, and on the desire to continue emitting, profiting, and consuming as usual – until at some point it became demonstrably clear that drastic emissions cuts were inevitable. And once that shift had occurred, we were no longer innocent, but were rather making the sometimes explicit, sometime implicit decision to accept the consequences of delayed action. We would continue to enjoy our easy ways, or – as might be argued by a neoclassical economist – we would delay the reckoning until we were more technologically advanced, and richer, and the costs of action would be lower and more bearable.

More issues arise when we try to choose an appropriate metric of responsibility. Bear in mind that we are actually concerned with two different impacts of greenhouse gas pollution – first, the *exhaustion* of the available "sinks," which has radically reduced the future opportunities of others to use those sinks, and second, the *harm* caused by greenhouse gas pollution. We must in both cases deal with complex links between emissions and impacts, and of course multiple gases. Even if we were concerned only with CO_2 emissions, we could choose to measure them, alternatively, as cumulative emissions over time, as the fraction of historical emissions that remain in the atmosphere, as the fraction of realized temperature change attributable to those emissions, or as the long-term contribution to expected temperature change. There are many issues here, and some are controversial (the inclusion of CO_2 emissions from deforestation first among them[27]), and no doubt countries will tend to favor definitions that favor their particular interests.

The critical question, though, from a "right to development" perspective, is *are all emissions created equal?* Should we count "survival" and "luxury" emissions in the same way?[28] Should CO_2 emissions from cooking and heating or methane emissions from subsistence rice agriculture be treated the same way as CO_2 from jet travel or CFCs from air conditioners? We argue that they should not be, that these different types of emissions are of fundamentally different natures, that, briefly, *survival emissions do not imply responsibility, whereas luxury emissions do*. We argue, moreover, that the recognition of this difference is critical to any burden-sharing framework designed to protect the right to development.

We argue, specifically, that safeguarding the right to development means allowing people to strive toward a decent level of economic development – the level defined by the development threshold – without being encumbered by emissions constraints. This will translate, as we go on to calculate indicative levels of national responsibility, into excluding those emissions that derive from a level of consumption below the development threshold.

Finally, as we did with capacity, we argue that the vast economic disparities within nations imply that responsibility must be conceived in a manner that recognizes the right to development as a right of individuals, not a right of countries. Even poor countries with overall low per capita levels of consumption and emissions have some residents who are members of the high-emitting consuming class. These emissions must be counted toward the country's responsibility, and hence its obligations.

3.3.3 Allocating obligations

Obligations, for their part, must be defined in a manner that combines capacity and responsibility. However this is done (and one sensible option is presented in Chapter 4), the underlying principle is clear. No national obligations should arise from the economic activities of individuals at low levels of development, as reckoned in terms of either wealth or emissions. Only when people cross the development threshold and enter the consuming class should their activities affect the obligations of the nation in which they live.

As it happens, most of the consuming class lives in the industrialized countries. And given our assumption that a true emergency program may have relatively high costs, the GDRs framework thus allocates obligations to industrialized countries that significantly exceed any levels that might currently be considered "realistic." But please note that it also assigns obligations to developing countries, and that, even though it specifies these obligations entirely by reference to the responsibility and capacity of their wealthier citizens, this assignment clearly violates a second principle of today's climate realism: that countries cannot be asked to incur any mitigation costs as long as they are "developing." So we hope that we have at least shown ourselves willing to be unrealistic on both sides of the great divide.[29]

The coal fired power plant in the background symbolizes the responsibility of industrialized countries for climate change, whereas the wind turbines represent their capacity to tackle it.

4 Quantifying the GDRs framework

In the preceding sections we described the urgency of the climate crisis and its implications for an emergency emissions reduction trajectory, and we drew conclusions about the nature of the burden-sharing system that will be needed in order to meet such a trajectory. In this section, we will estimate, step by step and quantitatively, the implications of the Greenhouse Development Rights approach. So recall that we have claimed that it is a reference framework, in that it lays out problems that must be solved by any viable climate regime. If this claim is true, this quantification is particularly useful, insofar as it highlights some stark – and we would claim inescapable – conclusions about who will have to pay to resolve the climate crisis.

At the core of the GDRs framework is the right to development, from which we seek to derive a consistent burden-sharing system that combines a measure of *responsibility* (historic contributions to greenhouse gas pollution) with a measure of *capacity* (broadly, the ability to pay for mitigation and adaptation). Crucially, these are defined in a manner that is sensitive to inequality *within* countries, which is to say that we treat nations as collections of economically unequal individuals. By so doing, we calculate national shares of the global mitigation and adaptation burden in a manner that, we believe, is truly consistent with the UNFCCC's broad principle of "common but differentiated responsibilities and respective capabilities."

We do not claim that this elaboration defines the only possible responsibility and capacity-based burden-sharing system. Our quantifications, in particular, necessarily bear elements of arbitrariness. But this will be true of all attempts to generate practical measures of ethically-based principles, and we do claim that the specific numeric choices and assumptions that we have made are consistent with the principles that they are intended to capture. We claim, that is, that our quantifications are fundamentally reasonable, that they indicate the *scale* of defensible national obligations, and that they usefully illustrate the qualities necessary to a climate regime that safeguards the right to development.

4.4 Steps to a Responsibility and Capacity Indicator

4.1.1 Calculating capacity

Quantifying capacity in a manner that accounts for intranational disparities in income, as defined with respect to a development threshold (as discussed in Section 3) is relatively straightforward. And the results can be illuminating. For example, Figure 3, below, is a "Capacity/Development Need" chart that compares three key countries – India, China and the United States – showing for each an estimated income distribution based on the national per capita income and Gini coefficient (a measure of national income inequality).[30] At each point on the x-axis, this curve shows the income of the corresponding percentile (1 percent) of the population, measured in US dollars per capita (PPP adjusted). Each chart shows the income rising from the poorest percentile to the wealthiest, and by so doing helpfully illustrates a few key concepts. (Note that the charts have been scaled so that the length of the x-axis is proportional to population, and thus the areas of the different sections – for example, the green section representing capacity – can be directly compared in absolute terms.)

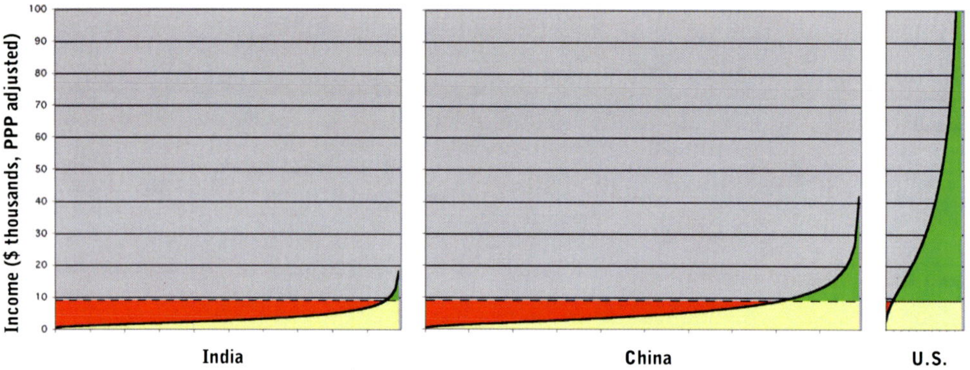

Figure 3. Capacity/Development Need chart for India, China and the United States, with $9,000 per capita (PPP) development threshold. See text.

One key concept illustrated here is the development threshold itself, which is shown as the dashed horizontal line at $9,000 that crosses the income distribution line and splits the population into a poorer portion (to the left) and a wealthier portion (to the right). Obviously, the precise point where such a line crosses that threshold depends on the wealth and income distribution of the country in question, but since all national populations include at least some people earning less than $9,000/year and some earning more, it always does. And since we are working with a global development threshold, this crossing makes it easy to compare both the heights of wealth and the depths of poverty in different countries. For each, the income needed to raise the poorer part of the population to the development threshold is reflected in the red area on the left side of the charts, an area bounded below by the income distribution curve and above by the threshold. We term this area the *development need*. The charts also graphically convey each country's *capacity*, which we define as the income that the wealthier portion of the population has above the development threshold. This we depict as the green area bounded below by the threshold and above by the income distribution curve. All in all, this approximation of capacity is a somewhat crude but still defensible representation of the national income that could legitimately be "taxed" to help shoulder the climate burden.

Consider India, shown in the left panel. By our calculations, more than 95 percent of the Indian people have incomes below the $9,000 development threshold. Plainly, in India as in similar countries, total national capacity – to pay for development, adaptation, or mitigation, or for that matter luxury consumption – is small compared to the national development need. Yet, just as plainly, India and other poor countries contain large (in absolute terms) middle classes and even a subclass of truly rich people (though these latter are so few as to be invisible in these low-resolution charts).[31]

The center panel of the chart shows China. It has much more capacity than India, both in absolute terms and relative to its development need, but note as well that about *80 percent of the Chinese population is still below the $9,000 threshold.* Clearly, China is not a wealthy country, not taken as a whole, though at the same time its absolute capacity is rather high, and the claim that shortages of investment capital (rather than consumption choices or institutional priorities) are limiting efforts at human development (and thus that few resources are available for climate mitigation) is not actually very credible.

Finally, on the right, we see the United States. Here, graphically, is an image of wealth. The "development need" of the small number of people with incomes under the threshold is entirely dwarfed by the "capacity" of the rest, however you choose to name or categorize them. Which is not to say that this need is in any way irrelevant, or tangential to our concerns. Indeed, the continued existence of injustice and vulnerability within the wealthy world (think of New Orleans) is a key political challenge to any international burden-sharing regime, in the sense that rich-world obligations must not be met at the expense of the rich-world poor. In any case, the financial capacity of Americans with incomes above the development threshold (the only income that counts toward the calculation of capacity) is extremely large, both absolutely and in relation to the national development need. Indeed, a good fraction of the US population has incomes so high that they are literally "off the charts."

These charts largely speak for themselves, but one point, at least, should be explicit. Even though GDRs attributes capacity to both poor and wealthy countries, its implications are quite different in these two cases. Poor countries, as befits their small capacity, have small obligations, which can be discharged entirely through domestic action. Wealthy countries will not generally have such an option, for as we will show, their obligations tend to be too great to be discharged with domestic action alone.

One consequence of this approach is that countries with the same population and the same average income do not necessarily have the same capacity, because a more *unequal* national income distribution will raise it. Consider two countries "Fairland" and "Unfairland," both with a population of one million people. In both, the per capita income is $5,000, but Fairland has a completely equal distribution of income (everyone makes $5,000), while in Unfairland, 98 percent of the population has an income of $3,000 and the other two percent has an income of $103,000. Now, clearly, the wealthy 2 percent of Unfairland's population is more able to pay taxes than the poor 98 percent, for they can pay them by reducing their luxury consumption. Indeed, they are more able to pay than any of the people of Fairland, where the people are all equally, relatively poor. Which is to say that, all else being equal, the more rich people in a country, the less sacrifice is required for a capacity-based tax or levy to raise the same amount of revenue.[32]

Using the method described above, Table 1 below shows the capacity for low-income, middle-income, and high-income countries (as per the World Bank's categories),[33] along with the share of global income, the share of global population, and the fraction of the population over the $9,000 development threshold in each group. Much can be read from this table, but note in particular that only 2.2 percent of the people in poor countries and 25 percent of the people in middle-income countries have incomes over the development threshold, and that the "capacity" of these countries (which together contain 84 percent of the global population) is *only 21 percent of the global total.*

	Low income	Middle income	High income	World
Income 2005 ($ trillion PPP)	6	23	33	62
Share of global income (percent)	9	37	54	100
Share of population 2005 (percent)	37	48	16	100
Per capita income 2005 ($ thousands PPP)	2.5	7.4	33.2	9.6
Capacity ($ trillion PPP)	0.2	6	24	31
Share of global capacity (percent)	0.5	20.7	79	100
Percentage of population over $9,000	2.2	25	93	27

Table 1. Characteristics of low-income, middle-income and high-income countries, including income, population and "capacity" as defined by $9,000 development threshold.

4.1.2 Calculating responsibility

As noted above, there is no uniquely "correct" or uncontroversial definition of responsibility. We suggest, however, that *cumulative per capita CO2 emissions from fossil fuel consumption since 1990* is a reasonable one, largely because emissions made prior to this date were usually (though not always) made in ignorance rather than by deliberate policy.

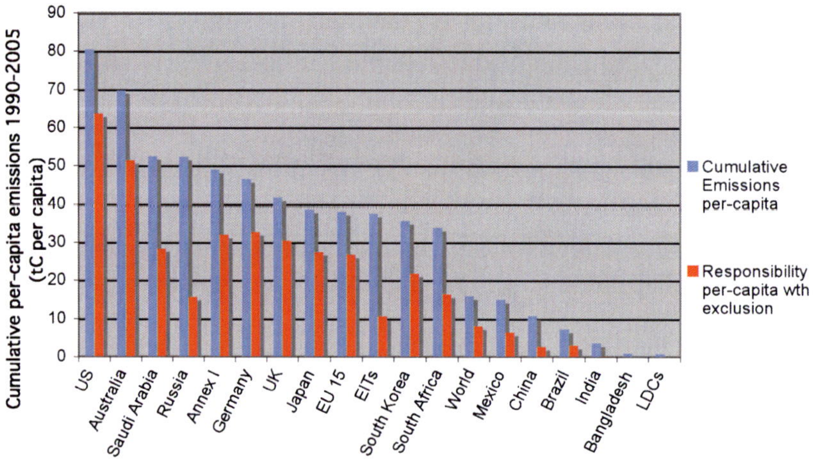

Figure 4. Cumulative per capita CO_2 emissions from fossil fuel combustion, 1990-2005 (in blue); "responsibility" adjusted to account for the exclusion of emissions below the development threshold (in red). (See the appendix for data sources and calculation details.)

Figure 4 shows this measure of responsibility for selected countries and regions; the blue bar is the total national per capita figure (from 1990 to 2005), while the red bar adjusts to account for the exclusion of emissions below the development threshold. The adjustment is straightforward, based on our assumption that (within any given country) emissions are proportional to consumption, which is, in turn, proportional to income (see the appendix for a technical discussion of these assumptions).

By this proxy, responsibility is, not surprisingly, higher in wealthy countries, and effectively zero in the poorest countries (including, but not limited, to the UN "Least

Developed Countries"). There are also important differences among countries with similar incomes. Some wealthy countries have much lower emissions than others (compare, for example, the United Kingdom or Japan with the United States), and some poor countries have much higher emissions than others (for example, Russia v. Mexico). This raises the question of how capacity and responsibility should be combined into a single obligation indicator capable of meaningfully driving the allocation of the global burden. We now turn to that question.

4.1.3 The Responsibility and Capacity Indicator (RCI)

To review: The goal of this indicative calculation is to define and calculate a single indicator that properly combines responsibility and capacity and, by so doing, allows us to defensibly assign shares of the global mitigation and adaptation burdens to individual countries. Further, this Responsibility and Capacity Indicator (RCI) must – following our claim that the right to development adheres to individuals and not nations – reflect the distribution of income and emissions within countries. When used to calculate national obligations, it should specifically exclude the responsibilities and capacities of individuals below the development threshold.

Again, there cannot be any uniquely correct way to do this, but there are more or less reasonable possibilities.[34] Plainly, the RCI must be defined so that, among countries with the same capacities but different responsibilities, the country with greater responsibility has the greater obligation. Just as plainly, among countries with the same responsibility but different capacities, the one with the greater capacity must have the greater obligation.

There are many formulas which have this property. We use one which multiplies responsibility and capacity, in a way that allows different weights to be given to each:

$$RCI = R^{a} \bullet C^{b}$$

We specify that the exponents a and b sum to 1, so that, as the paired weights go from a = 1 and b = 0 at one extreme to a = 0 and b = 1 at the other, the RCI goes from being exactly equal to responsibility (*R*) to being exactly equal to capacity (*C*). In our reference case, we set a = 0.4 and b = 0.6, which is to say that we weigh capacity somewhat higher than responsibility. Again, this is just one of many possible choices, but our belief is that it is less fair to make a poor nation with high emissions pay more than it is to make a rich country with low emissions pay more. But we show a sensitivity analysis in the appendix, and we fully expect that some people will prefer other formulas. A further explanation of how the calculations are done, taking account of income distributions, is given in the appendix.

By assuming that the national distribution of responsibility is the same as the national distribution of income (an oversimple assumption that is nevertheless reasonable for our purposes), we can straightforwardly estimate the joint responsibility/capacity indicator for any portion of the population. By integrating, we can then estimate the country's total RCI, and compare it with the global total to calculate each country's share. The results of this calculation for selected countries and groups of countries are shown in Table 2.

	Percentage share of					
	Global population	Global income	Global capacity	Cumulative emissions 1990–2005	Global responsibility	Global RCI
United States	4.7	20.2	31.8	23.7	37.0	34.3
EU (27)	7.7	21.5	29.0	17.8	23.1	26.6
United Kingdom	0.9	3.3	4.7	2.5	3.6	4.3
Germany	1.3	4.0	5.6	3.8	5.2	5.5
Russia	2.2	2.5	1.5	7.4	4.3	2.3
Brazil	2.9	2.6	2.1	1.3	1.0	1.6
China	20.4	14.7	7.1	13.8	6.6	7.0
India	17.0	6.1	0.4	3.8	0.3	0.3
South Africa	0.7	0.9	0.8	1.6	1.5	1.1
LDCs	8.3	1.4	0.1	0.4	0.0	0.0
All high income	15.6	53.9	78.8	52.7	76.9	78.5
All middle income	47.7	36.6	20.7	41.1	22.8	21.1
All low income	36.7	9.5	0.5	6.2	0.4	0.5

Table 2. Global percentage shares of population, income, capacity, cumulative emissions, responsibility and RCI for selected countries and groups of countries.

When reviewing this table, keep three basic points in mind:

1) Because our measure of capacity excludes the income of poor people, wherever they live, a rich country's capacity will be larger in percentage terms than its share of global income, and a poor country's capacity will be lower.
2) Similarly, though less transparently, a wealthy country's responsibility will be larger than its share of cumulative emissions. (Fewer of its historical emissions will be excluded.)
3) An indicator that combines responsibility and capacity to derive an obligation indicator can be expected to yield a result that is between the calculated capacity on the one hand and the calculated responsibility on the other. (As we weight capacity slightly higher than responsibility, our result is closer to the capacity number than to the responsibility number.)

One notable feature of our results is that the United States has the largest share of global capacity, the largest share of global responsibility and the largest share of combined RCI. We'll translate this into per capita terms shortly, after following a few more steps. However, this result is extremely important, and deserves immediate notice: *By any reasonable standard of "common but differentiated responsibilities," the United States would have to pay the largest share of the global climate "bill."* But, despite the fact that the American people have come to accept the need for concerted action to stabilize the climate, that action is still conceived in almost entirely domestic terms. Indeed, when it comes to preparing the ground for US international obligations, the American climate movement has largely failed, having barely begun to even explain the necessities of emergency global action to its people. The same, moreover, is true in Europe, though perhaps to a slightly lesser degree.

This is a harsh charge, so allow us to reiterate: It will not be enough for the wealthy countries to embark on an aggressive program of domestic reductions, not even if it is an *extremely* aggressive one. Their "bills" properly include much of the burden of accelerated *global* decarbonization, and of the robust adaptation program that will be needed if we are to maintain a workable measure of international solidarity and cooperation. But, thus far, the US and EU climate communities have generally failed to even raise these issues, let alone campaign on them. Obviously, this is a very serious problem.

Again, there is no single "correct" way to define a Responsibility and Capacity indicator. But we are confident that our definition is reasonable, and especially confident that its built-in sensitivity to the distribution of income and emissions within countries is crucially important. It is this sensitivity that takes account of the primal facts of income inequality: In every country, some people have the responsibility for unsustainable levels of greenhouse gas pollution, and the proportionate capacity to pay for mitigation and adaptation; in every country, some people have no responsibility and no capacity to pay. Any climate regime that seeks to honor the right to development must acknowledge, and internalize, these facts.

4.1.4 Calculating national "bills"

Having calculated RCIs for different countries, we can now estimate the obligations that would fall to specific countries. How those obligations would best be apportioned within countries is, of course, a different matter, though it would be contrary to the spirit of the GDRs system if, at the end of the day, the costs of climate protection were to devolve to those below the development threshold. The challenges here are great, but they are not specific to Greenhouse Development Rights. Any climate regime must ensure that, at a minimum, it neither worsens the overall fairness of the global economy or the overall well-being of the poor. If it does either, it is unlikely to survive.

In any case, our first task, if we are to use our RCIs to estimate national mitigation and adaptation costs, is to contrive reasonable estimates of the global costs that must be apportioned, and this despite a background of extreme uncertainty and confusion. (The UNFCCC has just reported it is own estimates, which are not wildly different from ours.[35]) The most widely cited numbers are for stabilization between 500 and 550 ppm CO_2-equivalent, and estimate the cost to be about of 1 percent of GWP (65 trillion US dollars in 2005) annually, although exactly how this number is defined is often a bit unclear in the literature.[36] Expected costs vary with baseline levels of economic and population growth and with assumptions about the efficiency with which policies will be implemented. And of course differences in basic definitions (what counts as a cost, and to whom?) and modeling assumptions produce different calculated costs, even with the same baseline and policy assumptions.

Our own view combines optimism and pessimism. That is to say, our understanding of the economic models leads us to conclude that the majority of them overstate costs relative to the mitigation objectives that they are actually modeling.[37] However, the scenario that we are advocating – an "emergency program" – demands rates of emissions reductions that are outside the range typically modeled (the lowest stabilization levels reported by the Fourth Assessment Report's Working Group III are 445–550 ppm CO_2-equivalent, whereas our "emergency pathway" aims to return to 400 ppm CO_2-e by 2100).

A more detailed discussion of mitigation costs would take us rather far afield, and in the end we would still be forced to conclude that there is enormous uncertainty, and little assurance of any specific upper bound to the costs of a true emergency program. Fortunately, for our purposes here, it is sufficient for us to use "reasonable numbers," and to stress that *the larger the burden turns out to be, the more crucial it is that it be shared fairly.*

More important still is the fact that *adaptation costs, properly conceived, may turn out to be as large or even larger than mitigation costs.* The burden-sharing literature rarely treats these costs seriously, but estimates in the region of $100 billion per year are being reported, though there is little basis for confidence.[38] Discussion about what kinds of adaptation measures are possible and desirable are just beginning, and there has yet to be any coherent proposal as to what kind and degree of adaptation would be "adequate," or of how "practical" proposals might be measured against such a standard. Even more importantly, discussions of adaptation have studiously avoided its inevitable relationship to liability and compensation. Yet lurking behind images of fresh new seawalls are increasingly clear understandings of the disaster relief and relocation costs that occur after a climate-change induced "impact" has occurred. Considering these factors, and the impacts that will be visited on both developed and developing countries, it is hardly farfetched to imagine global adaptation and compensation costs reaching or exceeding 1 percent of GWP each year.

We will not attempt to resolve the uncertainties here, but will rather proceed by estimating national bills for *each* 1 percent of GWP that we finally accept as part of the total climate burden. (Since our concern is to allocate that total burden – adaptation plus mitigation costs – we do not need to parse them out separately.) This 1 percent estimate can stand for a case in which both adaptation and mitigation costs are 0.5 percent of GWP, or a case in which one is 0.9 percent and the other 0.1 percent.

	Total income	Total capacity	Share of global RCI	If total mitigation and adaptation costs are 1 percent of GWP	
	($ billion PPP adjusted, 2005)	($ billion PPP adjusted, 2005)	(percent)	Total bill ($ billion PPP adjusted)	Average "taxpayer" bill ($ PPP/person)
United States	12,497	9,868	34.3	212	780
EU (27)	13,292	8,997	26.6	164	372
United Kingdom	2,004	1,466	4.3	26	458
Germany	2,472	1,735	5.5	34	428
Russia	1,552	464	2.3	14	194
Brazil	1,601	651	1.6	10	193
China	9,078	2,201	7.0	43	142
India	3,779	128	0.3	2.1	51
South Africa	525	253	1.1	6.5	382
LDCs	832	15	0.0	0.2	7
All high income	33,301	24,443	78.5	485	519
All mid. income	22,589	6,422	21.1	130	170
All low income	5,859	168	0.5	2.8	55
World	61,750	31,029	100.0	617	353

Table 3. Total national income and national capacity (calculated with a $9,000 development threshold), along with national and average "taxpayer" bills assuming a total global obligation (combining mitigation and adaptation) of 1 percent of GWP. A "taxpayer" is defined as a resident with an income above the development threshold; those with incomes below the threshold are assumed to pay nothing. Note that the United Kingdom and Germany are included in the EU27 figures, and also shown separately. (All figures 2005 US dollars, PPP-adjusted.)

In Table 3, we show national "bills," following the RCIs shown above and using this 1 percent of GWP cost estimate, for selected countries and regions. (This is done in terms of the 2005 GWP, 2005 being the latest year for which national data is readily available. In general, the three significant digits of precision here should not be taken too seriously.) In addition to showing the national obligation in billions of dollars, we also show an "average taxpayer bill" – the amount that (on average) would have to be paid by each person whose income was over the $9,000 development threshold in order to discharge the full national obligation. (These bills would obviously be lower if they were "per capita" bills computed on the basis of total national population rather than only the population above the development threshold, and this is especially true in poor countries.) The wide range of these bills reflects the widely different degrees of "taxpayer" responsibility and capacity in different countries; indeed it varies across countries by more than an order of magnitude.

Keep in mind that these estimates of national obligation to pay (the last two columns) reflect our indicative calculation of RCI and assumes that total costs (both mitigation and adaptation) would be 1 percent of GWP.[39] Actual costs may in the end be quite a bit higher, and its also possible to tell stories in which they would be lower, but in any case it is easy to do the arithmetic. If you believe, for example, that the total cost of an emergency climate stabilization program would be more like two percent of GWP, just multiply the numbers in the last two columns by two. Similarly, if you think the total cost is likely to be 0.5 percent, divide it in half.

Note, too, that these figures make no assumptions about the fraction of any national obligation that could reasonably be discharged domestically, as opposed to internationally. Nor have we sought to prejudge the institutional, political and governance mechanisms that would be necessary were such obligations to be codified in international law, collected and actually channeled toward mitigation and adaptation activities. That is, we have said next to nothing about how countries would actually pay their bills, or how their payments would be productively directed toward their targets. Certainly, one can imagine a great variety of mechanisms for generating the payments, such as various fees, levies, trade-related charges, carbon taxes and progressive income and/or consumption taxes. Similarly, one can imagine a great variety of mechanisms for directing the payments, such as funds, markets, incentives and such. But any real discussion of these issues is far beyond the scope of this paper. Suffice it to say that the problems here are inadequately understood and extremely daunting, and that they are not ours alone. In fact, they are shared by any climate regime that purports to actually do something about mitigation and adaptation.

Also, to move beyond the obvious point that these levels of "climate taxation" are not "realistic" it is useful to consider what they might appropriately be compared to. Military budgets in particular invite comparison. For example the US military budget, depending on what's included in its definition, is not less than $500 billion a year and, if estimated in a reasonable fashion, considerably more, as much as a third of the total US federal budget.[40] All other military budgets are smaller, but they still outweigh the climate costs assumed above. The United Kingdom's official military budget, for example, is about $51 billion a year, while China's is estimated at $188 billion and India's at $114 billion (all these figures are PPP). These are all conservatively estimated figures, and it is interesting to note that the military expenditures of the top 15 spenders amounts to just over 2 percent of GWP (PPP).[41] Given this, it is fair to say that an emergency program would entail a "Keynesian" effort of about the same size as the global military enterprise, though one that, obviously, follows a radically different storyline.

Finally, it is important to put these figures in the context of continuing global economic growth. As Azar and Schneider[42] among others have pointed out, even costs that seem very large – 2 percent of GWP, for example, is well over a trillion dollars – imply a very small delay in the rate at which people become richer. In a developed country growing at 2 percent a year, a 2 percent national bill would only mean a single year's delay in doubling current income, a delay from 2042 to 2043. And in a poor country growing at 5 percent annually, a 2 percent national bill would amount to less than a six-month delay in reaching such a milestone.

Working lunch of the G8 Heads of State and Government and the so-called Outreach representatives at the G8 Summit in Heiligendamm 2008

5 GDRs as a global allocation system

It might be useful to recall the purpose of this exercise – pulling "the right to development" down from the rhetorical skies and modeling an explicit burden-sharing system with that right at its core. Now, having defined a framework that might be able to support both rapid mitigation and, to the extent that it is possible, adaptation to limit the suffering and dislocation that will be caused by climate change, we believe that we have such a system in hand. We have even gone further, making reasonable estimates of the cost of mitigation and adaptation and using them to calculate implied "bills." For all this, however, we have said precious little about implementation, about collecting and distributing "ways and means," about actually carrying out a global emergency program. In this section, we explore one option: the implementation of the mitigation side of a GDRs system within an international "cap and allocate" trading system.*

This takes us, inevitably, into areas of bitter controversy. The institutions of modern economic life are so intimately bound up with the generation and globalization of inequality that even the suggestion that a fair international burden-sharing system can be instituted is controversial. And if such a system is to be market-based, skepticism is particularly warranted. If we may be frank, carbon-trading systems have had a rather inauspicious beginning. They have, in particular, shown themselves prone to "capture" by corporations and private traders, and this has in turn legitimated the fear, now extremely widespread, that any global emissions-trading system will function as a device by which wealthy countries, corporations and individuals can "buy their way out" of inconvenient emissions limitations.

Nevertheless, we think this exploration is warranted, for a number of reasons. First, the mitigation side of any global climate agreement is virtually guaranteed to involve market mechanisms, particularly in the critical years just ahead.[43] Such mechanisms, after all, have tremendous momentum and a large constituency – including carbon-intensive corporations, CDM project developers and hosts, the World Bank's Carbon Finance Unit, allowance-starved Annex 1 countries and finance-starved developing countries – that fully intend to move quickly into a next and grander phase of carbon trading. In this context, it seems to us vital to examine how the most promising form of international trading – a global cap and allocate system – could, if well designed and effectively regulated, help to support an emergency climate program.

---

* The term "cap and allocate" is shorthand for "cap and allocate and trade," and refers to any principle-based allocation of tradable allowances *to countries*, under a global cap. It is distinct from the (all too familiar) "cap and grandfather" systems, and there are many that continue patterns of historical inequity by formalizing rights to something (close to) historical emissions. Think of phase 1 of the EU's ETS.

Second, such a system would provide something of immense value: It would make it possible to achieve reductions *cost-effectively* by carrying them out wherever they were least expensive. Come what may, such cost effectiveness will be absolutely essential to the success of any true emergency program. Indeed, as the desperateness of our situation comes to be fully appreciated, we will be casting frenetically about for the most affordable ways to keep within the warming under control. And the lower the costs, the better the odds are that we will keep our resolve.

Third, and even more importantly, a workable "cap and allocate" system would make it possible to establish national mitigation obligations without regard to the volume of reductions that are physically (and economically) available within any given country. Trading, in other words, offers a way to implement a global burden-sharing system in which countries with high capacity and responsibility are obligated to carry out strenuous reductions at home *and also* to help pay for decarbonization in poorer countries. This is a key point, and we must underscore it, though we gladly add that, in principle, alternatives based on taxes, public funds and other financing mechanism could do the same. In any case, most of this section is devoted to the implications of such a burden-sharing system, which, trading-based or not, is our central concern.

5.1 Cap and allocate (and trade)

How then would we use the GDRs Responsibility and Capacity Indicator to distribute permits under a cap-and-allocate system? The means is fairly straightforward, and requires only three steps:

First, it is necessary to estimate the *global mitigation requirement*. This is the difference between a global baseline trajectory (constructed as a bottom-up aggregation of national baseline trajectories) and the emergency 2°C trajectory. Graphically, the "gap" or "wedge" between these two curves reflects the amount of mitigation work that needs to be done globally.

Second, this global mitigation requirement is divided into *national mitigation obligations*. Each country – however rich or poor it may be – is allocated a portion of the global mitigation requirement, in proportion to its aggregate national RCI.

Third, each country is assigned a *national emission budget* equal to its national baseline trajectory minus its national mitigation obligation. This determines each country's share of the (rapidly declining) global emissions budget, and makes it possible to assign each country an appropriate permit allocation (equal to its national emission budget).

Conceptually, this is akin to the original Brazilian proposal, which was intended to divide a global reduction requirement (relative to 1990 levels) among Annex I countries. In the rest of this section, we will follow the above steps in order to calculate future allocations for selected countries. But first note this critical point: Depending on the relationship between its baseline trajectory and its mitigation obligation, a country might have 1) an allocation allowing some emissions growth over time, 2) an allocation requiring a rate of emission reductions that could easily be met domestically, 3) an allocation requiring substantial domestic reductions *as well as* the purchase of permits from abroad. We will show examples illustrating the first and last of these cases.

One key clarification about national baseline paths is needed. In Figure 5 below, we show global emissions projections based on two hypothetical trajectories. The first (the top of the green wedge) is a "business-as-usual" trajectory, which extrapolates the historical approach to energy conservation, renewables, fossil fuel subsidies, pollution controls, etc.[44] The second (the top of the red wedge) is a so-called "no-regrets" trajectory, a projection of the global emissions pathway as it would be if all negative- and zero-cost emissions reductions were successfully captured.[45] The green wedge, in other words, represents free and profitable reductions, which are large, though not by any means large enough to bring emissions all the way down to the global emergency 2°C trajectory (the top of blue area).

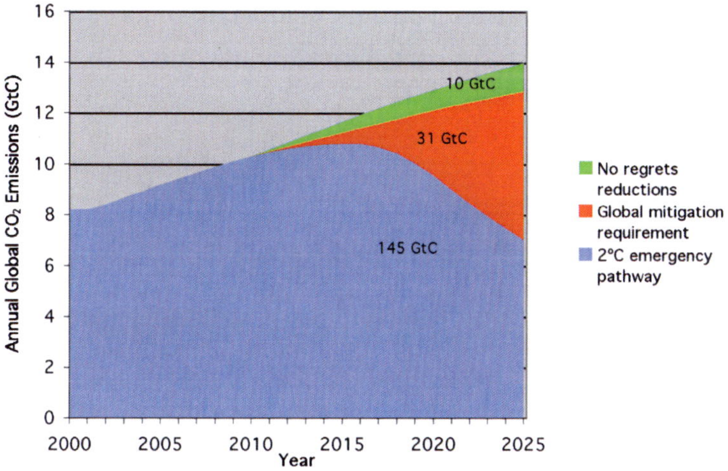

Figure 5. The "mitigation gap" (red wedge) between a "no regrets" baseline (border of red and green) and the 2°C emergency pathway (border of red and blue). See text.

We argue that a country's "no regrets" trajectory should be adopted as its national baseline. That is to say that all nations should be responsible for capturing their own "no regrets" reductions, and that only further reductions – those that actually cost something to realize – should count toward discharging a national mitigation obligation.

Baselines are, of course, notoriously difficult to define and impossible to accurately forecast. Thus, the negotiations would see plenty of gaming over such national baseline trajectories. But this, please note, is an inevitable feature of essentially all international burden-sharing proposals. In the face of any proposed commitment, negotiators carefully consider the levels of effort implied by their own prospects and those of other countries. Either explicitly or implicitly, they assess any effort relative to the "effortless" case. This will not change. But explicitly requiring each country to put forward a national "no regrets" trajectory, and then subjecting it to the scrutiny of international negotiations, would add transparency to a process that has to this point allowed discussions of national baselines, levels of effort and underlying principles to occur as a tangled, indecipherable mess.

Taking this "no regrets" definition of the baseline trajectory, Figure 5 shows the global mitigation requirement associated with the emergency program as the red wedge. Its width, growing through time, reflects the additional annual emissions reductions required to hold the 2°C line, relative to a world in which countries diligently work to capture the benefits of all "no regrets" opportunities. Given our baseline projections and our emergency pathway, the global mitigation burden over the period 2011–2025 would amount to 31 GtC of emissions reductions. This burden is then allocated to each nation in proportion to its share of the global RCI, as shown in Table 3 above.

Graphically, the global mitigation burden can be divided into wedges, as in Figure 6. These wedges are analogous to the technology-based wedges defined by Pacala and Socolow,[46] but instead of showing technologies and the gigatons of reductions that they are projected to deliver, they show countries and the gigatons of reductions they are obligated to pay for. Thus the United States' wedge is 35 percent of 31 GtC, or about 11 GtC, while the European Union's wedge (including the British and German shares, which are here shown separately) is 27 percent, a bit below 8 GtC. Russia, a middle-income country, gets 2.3 percent, or 0.7 GtC, and China, another, gets 6.9 percent, or 2.1 GtC.

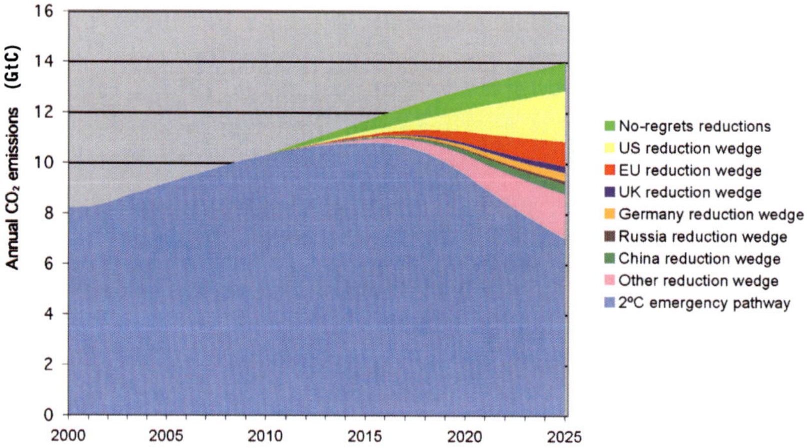

Figure 6. Mitigation requirement, divided into "obligation wedges" that reflect national / regional shares of RCI. (The United Kingdom and Germany are of course part of the European Union, but are shown separately here; total EU obligation is thus shown as a three-color wedge.)

This gives us the big picture, in a way that sets us up to talk, usefully and quantitatively, about individual national situations. For example, we can "zoom in" on a country to look at its mitigation obligation wedge – its share of the necessary global reductions – and compare this wedge to its national "no regrets" trajectory. And we can examine the relationship between its plausible rates of *domestic emissions reductions* and the scale of its total mitigation obligation, and thus specify the *international reduction* it would need to somehow subsidize to fulfill its obligation.

Such examinations can be quite striking, for they plainly show that wealthier countries with high RCIs are obligated to deliver reductions far larger than even the ambitious 90 percent by 2050 targets now being discussed (at least by Al Gore and a few others) for Annex 1 countries. Indeed, for key wealthy countries, *reduction obligations exceed even total baseline emissions. So that even if these countries were to reduce their emissions to zero, they would still be obligated to pay for emissions reductions elsewhere.*

This result, though striking, is not at all surprising. In fact, it exists by design. It is the intended outcome of the fact – for it is a fact – that any framework that actually preserves the right to development must obligate the wealthy nations to rapidly reduce their own emissions at the same time as they pay to accelerate the decarbonization of the developing world. And it follows, equally implacably, from an allocation of reduction obligations on the basis of responsibility and capacity. It is the reason that Greenhouse Development Rights works, the way it drives global decarbonization, the means by which it creates the atmospheric space needed by those who are still "underdeveloped."

The example of the United Kingdom is given below in Figure 7.

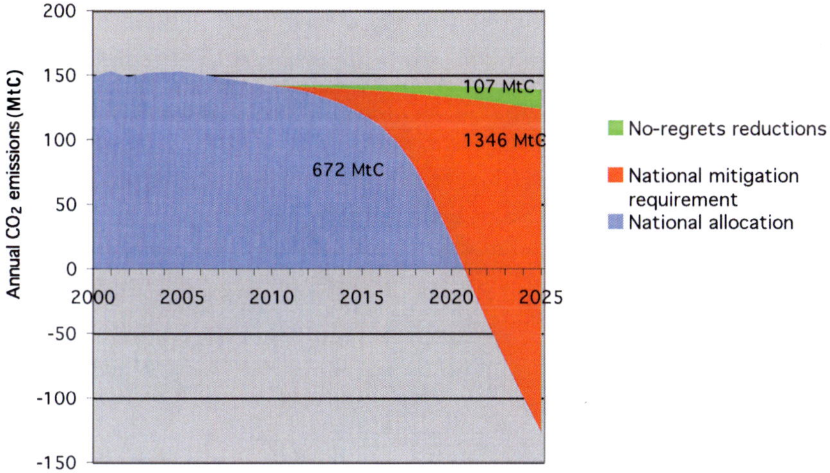

Figure 7. "Mitigation Obligation" chart for the United Kingdom for the period 2010–2025. See text.

The top line, at the top of the green wedge, represents the "business-as-usual" case (emissions growth as per the IPCC's A1B scenario), while the lower border of the green wedge shows the United Kingdom's "no regrets" trajectory, calculated on the basis of the IPCC B1 scenario's projected growth rate for OECD countries. The green wedge, in other words, is an estimate of the United Kingdom's "no regrets" reductions opportunities between 2010-2025, which here amounts to 107 MtC, all of which is the responsibility of the United Kingdom to aggressively exploit. The striking bit, though, is the red wedge. It represents the United Kingdom's share of the global mitigation requirement, its national reduction obligation, which amounts, under our assumptions, to 1368 MtC. Thus, the lower border of the red wedge shows the United Kingdom's effective allocation, once its national mitigation obligation has been subtracted from its "no regrets" trajectory. (The allocation is here shown as a pathway in time, although it might, in practice, be better assigned as a cumulative allocation over the 15-year (2011 to 2025) "commitment period" shown.)

Although this chart looks quite different from the above global chart (Figure 6), this is entirely due to the scale of the axes; both show the United Kingdom's same 1368 MtC mitigation obligation "wedge." The real difference is that, this time, this wedge in the spotlight, and its significance is more obvious because it is shown relative to the United Kingdom's emissions, not global emissions. Given this, the way the "allocation" line drops below zero around 2021 is pretty hard to miss, as is the political implication of this drop – the United Kingdom's mitigation obligation is not limited by the magnitude of its current emissions!

It is notable, in this context, that the GDRs framework makes no intrinsic assumptions about the combination of *domestic reductions* and *international reductions* that a country will choose in seeking to fulfill its mitigation obligations. With international purchases managed via a global cap and allocate system, a country would, at least in theory, be free to make any portion of its reductions domestically, and the remainder internationally, based on any nationally salient economic or political considerations. In practice, however, some restrictions are likely to be necessary, a point to which we will return below.

For the meantime, consider a scenario in which the United Kingdom's rate of domestic reductions mirrors the rate of global reductions demanded by the emergency 2°C pathway, which increase gradually after the 2015 global emissions peak and reaches a maximum of about 6 percent per year. The implications of this are illustrated below in Figure 8, wherein a yellow wedge, representing domestic reductions that accelerate at that same rate, is carved out of the United Kingdom's mitigation obligation. This yellow wedge represents 424 MtC of domestic physical reductions, and leaves the United Kingdom with a need to purchase or otherwise fund an additional 945 MtC of reductions internationally (the red wedge).

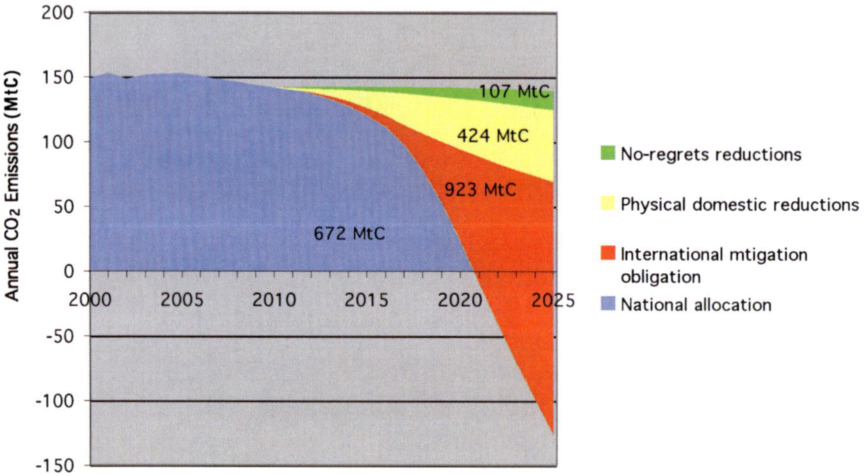

Figure 8. Hypothetical UK emissions reductions allocated between domestic reductions reaching a 6 percent annual rate of decline (yellow wedge), and international reduction obligations (red wedge) under the GDRs framework.

A greater rate of domestic reductions would, of course, reduce the United Kingdom's need to purchase offshore reductions. And, conversely, the United Kingdom could, at least in theory, refuse to make any reductions domestically, and to choose instead to purchase all its required reductions internationally. This latter approach, however, would be implausible, or irrational, or both, given that domestic reduction opportunities would accumulate unused while the national expenditure on internationally purchased reductions would grow more and more taxing. Still, the possibility is worth considering, for it raises the specter that the United Kingdom – or any other wealthy nation – could "buy its way out" of the need to make inconvenient domestic accommodations to the climate crisis. Such a choice would be both ethically problematic and politically dangerous, issues we will return to at the end of this section.

What this scenario illustrates – and indeed doing so is a major point of this entire exercise – is that even very steep domestic emissions reductions would only discharge a fraction of the mitigation obligations that, under a reasonable calculation of national responsibility and capacity, would properly fall upon the wealthy countries. This, again, is striking but not surprising. The underlying premise of the Greenhouse Development Rights framework is that the right to development must be safeguarded, and that doing so requires the world's wealthier population to both free up sufficient space for the poorer nations and subsidize their rapid transition to low-carbon economies. The need for the United Kingdom to make steep domestic reductions and still pay for major reductions internationally is merely the logical outcome of this foundational premise.

5.2 The example of the United States

In Figure 9 we show a similar calculation for the United States. But rather than a domestic reduction wedge that thickens to 6 percent per year (reflecting the global reduction rate in the emergency 2°C trajectory), we show an even more ambitious domestic reduction trajectory – call it Gore's trajectory – that reduces national emissions to 90 percent below 1990 levels in 2050.

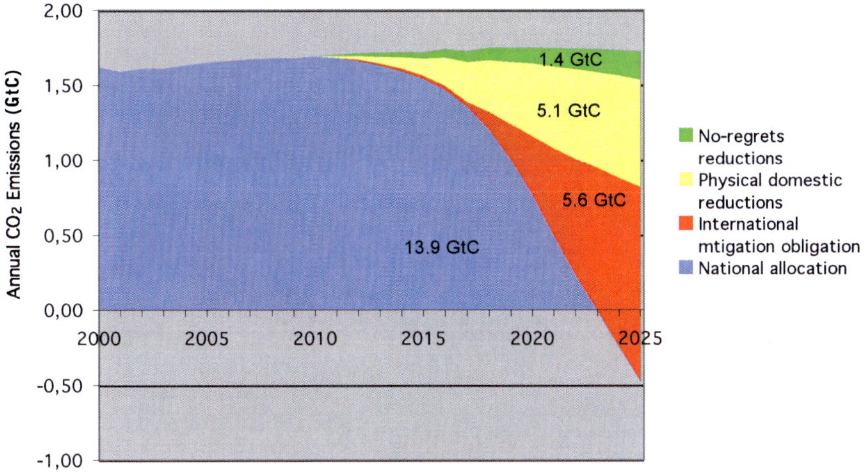

Figure 9. US allocation under GDRs reference case, with domestic physical reductions (yellow wedge) defined to (following Gore) reduce US emissions by 90 percent by 2050. See text.

In this "90 percent by 2050" trajectory, the rate of domestic emissions reductions reaches 6.7 percent annually by 2025, and leads to about five GtC of domestic reductions over the period of 2011 to 2025. This reduction rate is greater than those mandated by even the strictest of the bills now in play in the US Congress: the House of Representative's *Safe Climate Act* and the Senate's *Global Warming Pollution Reduction Act*. And, again, even these rapid reductions would only satisfy a portion of the United States' total obligation, the rest of which would have to be met by funding additional international reductions.

Which is as fine an opportunity as any to note that GDRs would substantially reframe the "international offsets" debate. Today, that debate turns on the limits that should, or should not, be placed on the ability of wealthy countries to purchase offshore reductions. The GDRs approach, however, implies that rich nations have reduction obligations that are quite properly *larger* than their plausible domestic reductions. The implication is that it is inevitable, and even desirable, for wealthy nations to pay for international reductions, and that the debate should focus not on limiting such payments but rather on ensuring that they are made in as fair and effective a manner as possible.

5.3 The example of Germany

The German case is also interesting. The top of the green wedge, again, represents "business as usual," while its lower border shows Germany's "no regrets" trajectory, calculated on the basis of the IPCC B1 scenario's growth rate for OECD countries. Here, as with the United Kingdom above, the rate of domestic reductions mirrors the global reductions demanded by the emergency 2°C pathway, which reach their maximum at about 6 percent per year). The implications of this are illustrated in Figure 10, wherein a yellow wedge, representing domestic reductions, is carved out of Germany's mitigation obligation. This yellow wedge represents 690 MtC of domestic reductions, and leaves Germany with a need to purchase or otherwise fund an additional 1032 MtC of reductions internationally (the red wedge).

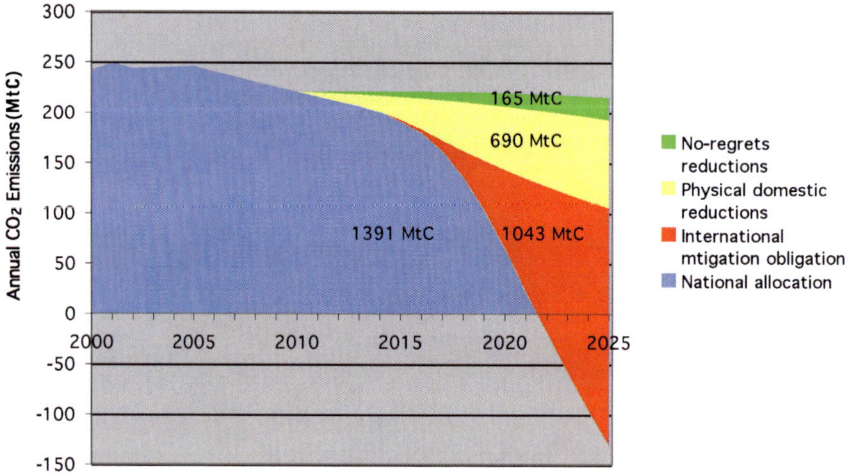

Figure 10. Hypothetical German emissions reductions allocated between domestic reductions reaching a 6 percent annual rate of decline (yellow wedge), and international reduction obligations (red wedge) under the GDRs framework.

5.4 The example of China

The complement to the situations illustrated above is the one in the developing world, where mitigation obligations are *smaller* than the 6 percent per annum reductions that would need to be maintained globally to hold the emergency 2°C trajectory. This situation is well illustrated by the case of China.

Here, again, the green wedge represents "no regrets" reductions. The "business-as-usual" trajectory (the top of the green wedge) is taken as an extrapolation of China's historical emissions growth, a choice that seems appropriate given its atypical rate and recent momentum, though the bottom of China's "no regrets" wedge, and thus its area, is still based upon the B1 emissions trajectory. But note that China's (yellow) mitigation obligation, calculated as it is on the basis of China's RCI, is still not particularly large, and this despite the projected continuation of China's unusually rapid economic growth.[47]

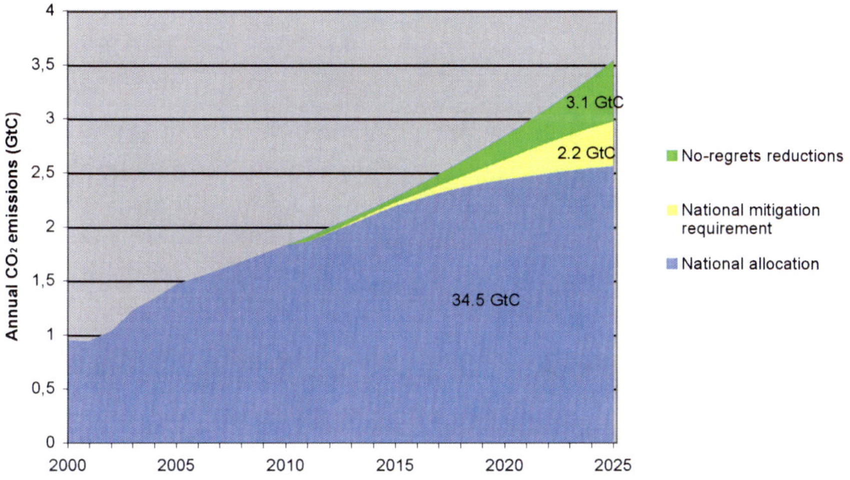

Figure 11. Allocation under GDRs framework reference case for China.

Finally, in Figure 12, below, we see the point of this story – a hypothetical instance in which large additional emissions reductions (the red wedge) are made within China, but financed by wealthy countries in need of offsets. These reductions are absolutely necessary, for China's emissions are large, and making full use of its mitigation potential is essential if we are to keep within the emergency 2°C trajectory. Fortunately, under the GDRs framework, there is a strong incentive for China to reduce beyond its national obligation by, in effect, selling mitigation potential to wealthy and middle-income countries like the United Kingdom and United States that need it to fulfill their mitigation obligations. Or, to put it another way, in a cap and allocate system, China would in principle be able to sell reductions at an international price that is greater than its marginal cost, and by so doing earn the revenue needed to finance its own required reductions, at least partially and perhaps wholly.

5.5 The trouble with carbon markets

The prospect of international carbon trading is controversial, and even divisive.[48] But as argued above, some kind of trading may well be inevitable, and, in the proper framework, desirable as well. Having said this, however, caveats are immediately necessary. Carbon-trading systems must be well designed, well implemented and well regulated. And a tough-minded, sustained effort must be made to ensure that, at the end of the day, they deliver on their promise of generating reductions – *real* reductions – cost-effectively. Cheap but illusory offsets (many of which are being provided by the Clean

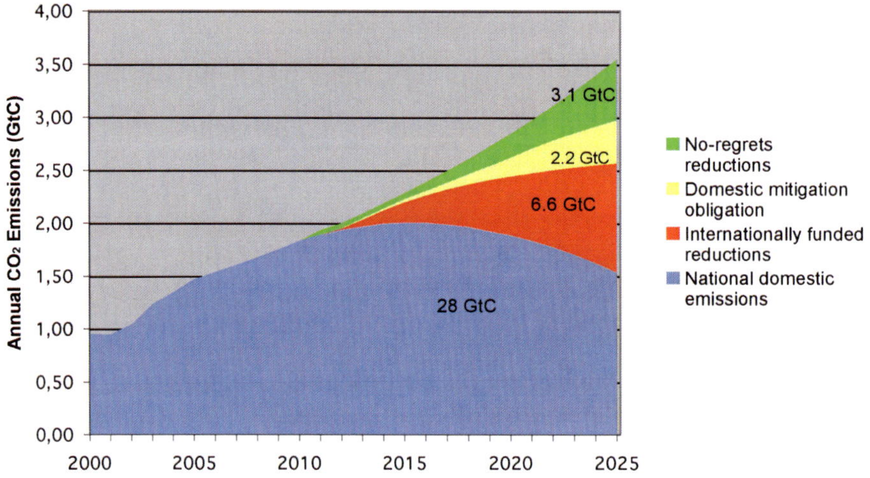

Figure 12. Plausible emissions trajectory for China under GDRs reference case if international purchases lead to 6 percent annual rate of reduction. See text.

Development Mechanism) are not a viable substitute. And it is not just the CDM that is a problem. The European Union's Emissions Trading System is crippled by grandfathering and over-generous allocations, and private carbon markets are a veritable Wild West of unsubstantiated reductions. All things considered, carbon-trading has not been going well, and, at this point, the onus is on the policymakers to prove that they are capable of designing and implementing trading systems that can be widely accepted as being both legitimate and useful.

Also, effective and broadly participatory social and environmental safeguards must be built into trading systems. However, this need is not limited to carbon markets or crediting systems. Any mechanisms that serve to channel large financial flows will be difficult to get right, and however they are structured, a great deal of civil-society and governmental involvement and oversight will be necessary s if they are to be both fair and effective. So whatever institutions we finally choose to mediate and manage the considerable international financial transfers that must, inevitably, be associated with a viable emergency program – whether these mechanisms are fund-based or tax-based or trading-based, whether they are public or private, whether they are tied to existing institutions like the World Bank or to the new institutions that the climate regime will inevitably call into existence – they will carry real risks. In every case, questions must be asked: about how the mechanisms work; about how transparent and accountable they are; about what strings are attached to them, and who is pulling these strings; about social and environmental safeguards; about governance. About who is hurt, who benefits, and who decides.

All this is critical because, whatever we do, some people will be negatively affected by the greenhouse transition. Mitigation and even adaptation will have their winners and losers, and the costs to the losers cannot be blithely ignored in the interests of some putative larger good. Indeed, any claims to a larger good must, finally, be judged in terms of affected peoples, and whether they have real opportunities to assert their interests, and to decide how these interests are understood and acted upon.

5.5.1 Setting limits

One key justification for emissions trading is that it allows nations to choose how much of their mitigation obligation they will discharge domestically, and how much internationally. And this is extremely relevant here, for the fact that countries may have obligations greater than their plausible rates of physical reductions – and possibly even greater than their total emissions – is central to the GDRs framework. It is by exercising their option to meet some of their obligations internationally, by paying for reductions in poor countries, that wealthy countries subsidize global decarbonization and leapfrogging.

But can this option be abused? What if wealthy countries try to "buy their way out" of the climate problem, by purchasing all or even most of their reductions internationally? To some degree, the emergency program contains a built-in corrective to this problem, since domestic reductions within wealthy countries would rapidly become difficult to pass up as the pressures of the 2°C trajectory bear down and reductions in the South become more costly. But what if this is not enough? After all, any true emergency program will inevitably, at some point, require serious structural adjustments (on top of major technological changes), and would wealthy northerners not be willing to pay quite a premium to avoid such adjustments and preserve their high-carbon lifestyles?

There are several issues here. One has to do with the path dependency of the carbon transition itself, which requires deep infrastructural change to start early and unfold over a long period of time (for example, more compact urban forms to reduce transport requirements). Such changes will not be universally popular, and wealthy countries might indeed seek to dodge the resulting discord by avoiding domestic reductions in favor of purchased international reductions. Such a strategy, however, would be extremely short-sighted. Internationally purchased permits will almost certainly continue to rise in price, and at some point might simply become too scarce to be affordable. At that point, wealthy communities that have failed to take the necessary early, incremental actions would be sorely temped to default on their obligations under the climate regime. And if they do, the regime, and the emergency program, would be in deep trouble.

A second problem arises from the reality of markets in an unequal world. The idealized view of emissions markets assumes that the sellers of permits are acting voluntarily, and perhaps even reaping a handsome profit. But, in fact, markets of all sorts engage actors with widely disparate levels of power. In this context, it is not always easy to ensure that the permits being sold by the South, or rather the mitigation that these permits correspond to, arise from the implementation of low-carbon energy services, rather than from the involuntary sacrifice of energy services (and hence welfare) by politically weak communities that are not being sufficiently compensated, or compensated at all.

Finally, politics matters. Under the rigors of an emergency program, high levels of international cooperation and solidarity will be essential, and it is extremely unlikely that these can be sustained if wealthy countries are seen to be buying environmental space in order to prolong their enjoyment of high-emitting lifestyles. Nor is it structurally advisable for them to do so. Since it is unlikely that technological changes alone will be able to deliver the needed rates of emissions reductions, the historically wealthy and high-emitting countries will have to help pioneer new kinds of low-impact lifestyles, of a kind that could be scaled up and be at least potentially adoptable by the growing global population. There is no way around it; this is not a story in which legitimacy and perceived justice are mere expendable ingredients.

These various arguments suggest that it might be justified to compel northern countries to make domestic reductions of at least the same scale as those required globally. That is, that it might be justified, under an emergency program, to compel nations with large national reduction obligations to make domestic reductions of at least 6 percent annually. Such a "supplementarity rule" would, to be sure, offend the economists, but this does not seem, on balance, to be a decisive argument against it. And given the inauspicious experience with carbon markets so far, the case for such a "regulatory backstop" is strong.

In any event, any climate regime that safeguards the right to development will have to provide a way for large amounts of resources to flow from the wealthy countries to the poor. This is the only way that the required mitigation can become a reality in time. Perhaps there are better ways than trading to achieve this objective. We shall see. In the meanwhile, we are compelled to admit that such international transfers will be difficult to achieve, and that, nevertheless, we must at all costs achieve them. Any climate regime that functions as just another brick in the wall of economic stratification will be rejected, and justly so.

Delegates gather in the plenary session on the final day of negotiations at the United Nations Climate Change Conference in Nairobi, Friday, 17 November, 2006.

6 Politics and Greenhouse Development Rights

The real world, of course, follows a more complex and varied path than can be represented by this sort of top-down analysis. Some recent developments, however, are directly relevant to our argument, and among these we would count sharpening disagreements within both Annex 1 and the G77/China; the emergence of the "Accession" or "+5" group (as in the "G8+5") of high-emitting developing countries (China, India, Brazil, South Africa and Mexico), and, of course, China's rising emissions. The United States, too, deserves special mention, particularly because, now in the late days of the Bush administration, the air is charged with the expectation of change. We all feel it, as we all, inevitably, hope for the best.

This hope could be easily dashed. The United States' obligation, after all, is uncomfortably high. Indeed, it is the highest in the world, as it will be by any reasonable responsibility- and capacity-based obligation indicator. And this reality will not be welcomed in even a Democrat-controlled Washington, or indeed within the average American household. So, yes, much will change when the Democrats take office, but it is not obvious that they will change enough to bring the United States into the new "leadership" position that so many people are hoping for. Because at this point, frankly, such leadership can only flow from an acceptance of national obligations, and from the promotion of approaches that take proper account of not only the scale and severity of the climate threat, but also the realities of unequal development.

The situation is changing fast. But even with "aspirational targets" such as "90 percent by 2050" on the rhetorical table, the imperatives of the short term are still the main drivers of climate policy. One way to put this is that there is no obvious way to be "policy relevant" while calling for an international framework designed to support a true emergency program. Soon, perhaps, this will change, but for the moment, Greenhouse Development Rights can only be a reference framework. As such, the tests of its utility are obvious enough: Does it help us to see where we actually are? Does it point beyond the short comings of existing climate policy? These are the important questions.

We, for our parts, believe that, by outlining a burden-sharing system appropriate to a twice-divided world, the Greenhouse Development Rights framework can serve as a useful and clarifying point of reference. That, at the least, it can help to call attention back to the rich/poor division, which has become altogether too obscure within the negotiations. This is particularly important when it comes to the large developing countries. For their challenge to the world lies not merely in their size – as if China, and India, and Brazil, despite their relative poverty, were the culpable ones – but is rather that, by their very size and dynamism, they stand between the rich world and the poor, and at the edge of an impossible future. The core of the impasse? Simply that there is very little atmospheric space left, far too little for the poor to "develop" along anything like the business-as-usual path, not at least if we are to avoid a catastrophe. And that, despite this and despite all else, the emerging powers of the South have no intention of abating their drive to development.

6.1 The showdown

Recall the June 2007 meeting of the G8+5. And recall that the battle there was one of targets and timetables. The drama was high but the plot, alas, was all too familiar. It was Angela Merkel's progressive Europe v. George Bush's self-interested America, and each came brandishing its favorite standards. Merkel spoke for a global emissions target of 50 percent reductions by 2050, which she presented as if it was unambiguously consistent with the 2°C temperature target. And, of course, the Bush administration replied, as everyone knew it would, with high-sounding refusal and twisted objections: What about China? What about India? What about the developing world?

These, unfortunately, are good questions. And they are questions that the European Union, for all its many attempts to move the agenda forward, has never satisfactorily answered. Which brings us to the point of this section – that from the GDRs perspective, the key lesson of 2007's G8+5 was not that the European Union could not move the Bush delegation, but rather that, even in the face of extreme provocation by the Americans, it could not even move the +5 countries. It was that China, India and the others did so little to support the Europeans. That, even as the European Union led a critical battle against an extremely unpopular US administration, the +5 countries barely left the sidelines.

So, why not?

Is it that southern negotiators do not believe the science? That they do not know how horrifically climate change will strike their nations, their lands, their vulnerable poor? Perhaps this is part of the story, but it does not really explain the singular reticence of the South's negotiators. Far better, we feel, to presume that they indeed understand the urgency of the climate crisis, but that they also understand its defining political reality. Which is that the emergency is now clearly on the table, along with loud calls for rapid, painfully stringent global reductions, but without any correspondingly serious protections for the South's developmental equity. That, in particular, the negotiations are characterized by a pervasive and critical absence of concrete proposals for a burden-sharing architecture that is capable of supporting rapid emissions reductions without radically circumscribing the prospects of the South's nations and populations. In fact, we believe that the South's negotiators – many of them at least – have consciously judged the situation, and, for better or for worse, have reached the conclusion that, absent substantive movement toward a defensibly fair global burden-sharing system, they have more to lose than to gain by admitting the severity of the crisis.

Such an interpretation will not, perhaps, be particularly controversial within the climate community. But it seems to us that neither its implications nor its explanatory power have been followed though. And this despite its ability to explain why the developing countries have been so consistent in not only rejecting the need for hard global targets, but also in resisting official recognition of the science (as, for example, China did during the drafting of the IPCC's recent Working Group I *Summary for Policymakers*) and, more generally, denying that humanity as a whole now faces an emergency situation. An emergency, after all, is by definition a situation that requires an extraordinary response, and southern decision-makers can be forgiven if, surveying the state of the real geo-political world and the lessons of the recent past, they conclude that a politics of global climate emergency would likely play out in a manner that constrains their developmental aspirations.

Nor is it obvious that they are wrong to do so.

It is helpful to illustrate the situation with one last set of graphs. Recall first Figure 2, from Section 3 above, which showed that developing country emissions alone will soon send us all hurtling across the 2°C line (and this even if the world was to follow the relatively benign pathway defined by the IPCC's B1 scenario family[49]). Indeed, if we define the 2°C line in terms of our emergency pathway (the one in which global emissions drop to 80 percent below 1990 levels in 2050, the one that has the highest probability of actually holding that line), developing-country emissions cross it in only about 15 years. And in even the least stringent of our pathways it would be crossed within 25 years.

Thus, even such a "relatively benign" pathway would likely wreak havoc. Instead, if we are to have a significant chance of holding the 2°C line, the developing world's emissions must, and exactly as its negotiators fear, drop extremely quickly. How quickly? Well, what if, just hypothetically, the Annex 1 countries were to commit to our emergency pathway, and what if, to prove their earnestness, they were to commit as well to the challenge of the day, making 90 percent reductions from the 1990 baseline by 2050? How much space would then remain for the development of the non-Annex 1 countries?

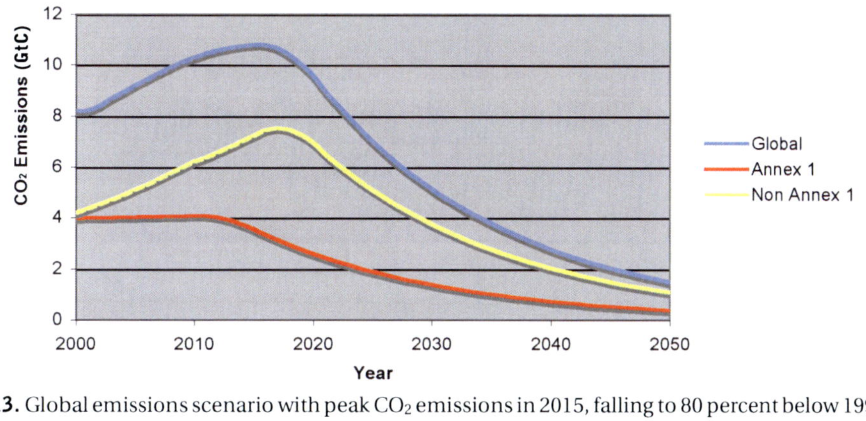

Figure 13. Global emissions scenario with peak CO_2 emissions in 2015, falling to 80 percent below 1990 levels in 2050. Annex 1 emissions decline to 90 percent below 1990 levels in 2050.

The math, alas, is implacable. In fact, as Figure 13 clearly shows, non-Annex 1 must itself be on an emergency path if we are to hold to the global emergency trajectory. Indeed, despite the rapid and deep cuts shown here in Annex 1, non-Annex 1 emissions would still have to peak *before* 2020, and still have to be dropping at 6 percent annually within a few years.

The problem is that, with only a small amount of emissions space left, there are few degrees of freedom available to allow for a more relaxed southern trajectory. The non-Annex 1 peak could be postponed, but only by committing to an even steeper subsequent decline. And, conversely, the decline could be less steep, but only if the peak was lower and came sooner. Neither of these alternatives is significantly more forgiving than the non-Annex 1 path shown in Figure 13. The other option, in theory, is that the North would make more space available. But this is already a scenario of extremely aggressive northern reductions, with 2050 emissions being cut by 90 percent. And even 100 percent would not open a great deal more space for the developing world. The possibility of emissions from the North going radically negative is in principle an option, but as discussed earlier, it is a distant option which cannot support our hopes.

The same trajectories are shown in per capita terms in Figure 14, which illustrates a different aspect of this same situation. Here we see that Annex I per capita emissions would decline dramatically in meeting this "90 percent by 2050" trajectory, but that even this would leave little space for non-Annex I to develop. In fact, non-Annex 1 per capita emissions would still have to drop sharply within the next few years, and this despite being a mere half of the northern average. That northern average would also drop of course, but it would remain far higher than the average in the South, and continue to reflect a far higher level of consumption. Consider, for example, India. Even assuming a steady 5 percent rate of annual growth (the average over the last 10 years), its per capita income would still be under $8,000 (PPP) in 2020. [50]

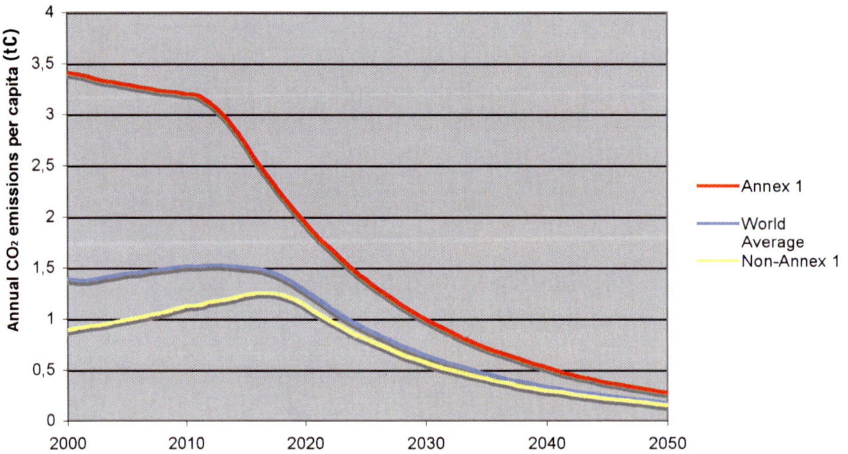

Figure 14. Per capita emissions (from fossil fuel combustion) in the emergency scenario with Annex 1 emissions declining to 90 percent below 1990 levels in 2050.

More could be said along these lines, but the point should be clear enough, and sufficient to illustrate why developing countries are so hesitant to commit to the 2°C target. Because if we are to have a real chance of keeping to that target, southern emissions simply *must* peak by around 2020, and then begin dropping by something like 6 percent a year. But all this seems to leave to the developing nations is a stifling "Contraction and Convergence" style future in which even efforts to modestly expand energy services knock quickly against inexorable limits, while the world's wealthy, by dint of their fortunately history, continue to enjoy luxury levels of consumption and emissions. And what this promises the South, or seems to, is a future in which developmental equity remains forever out of reach.

Fortunately, there are actually two possibilities. The first, as noted above, is one in which the climate crisis threatens to lock the South into a position of long-term underdevelopment, but it should be obvious by now that such a prospect can only harden the impasse and, by so doing, draw us further toward catastrophe. It is not a real option. The second, better possibility is that the threat of long-term underdevelopment can be taken off the table. Which means that the wealthy have to commit to a future in which global development no longer depends on rising emissions and then do whatever it takes to make that future real, in which developmental justice is understood not as a matter of equalizing per capita emissions but as a matter of extremely rapid global decarbonization. Such a program would have to be conceived, *and announced*, as one in which the poor – most of whom live in the South – are not obliged to pay.

This is the only way, and just the problem. Because right now such a global program simply is not on the agenda, and chances are pretty good that it is going to be hard to get it there. Which means that the developing countries, were they to commit to an emergency global emissions pathway, would be opening themselves to an entanglement that was likely to seriously compromise their development.

None of which is to say that the long battle to establish the 2°C target was a mistake. In fact, it was essential; the 2°C target is a proxy for the science as a whole, and expresses the emergency in a manner as clear as it is bracing. Nor is it correct to insist that a comprehensive, structurally appropriate burden-sharing regime (something like the GDRs framework) can now find real international traction. Clearly, we are not there yet. But, on the other hand, it is fair to say that we, all of us, including southern negotiators, have got to become a great deal more honest about the political logic of this extremely difficult situation, in which an emergency target is on the table, but without any accompanying burden-sharing architecture. This absence is a decisive one, and given it, we should not be surprised if vague talk about "no-lose" targets is not enough to move the +5 countries off the sidelines and into the ranks of the climate protection coalition.

Not to excuse the inaction in the North, but we are compelled to add that the southern negotiators are clearly part of the problem. For while emergency action really is impossible without a burden-sharing system that protects the right to development, *the South's negotiators have passed up numerous opportunities to put just such a system onto the table.* This must be recognized, because if any single move has a real chance of breaking the impasse, it would be *a southern proposal for an emergency architecture that the large developing countries could actually agree to.* So, though it might seem dangerous to engage with this almost impossible problem, it is time, past time really, for the South to step forward with just such a proposal.

6.2 Beyond the annexes

Whatever happens, an emergency program must come soon. In the meanwhile, we believe that the GDRs framework usefully clarifies the structure of the climate problem, and that it suggests bridges to the future. One such bridge, we believe, is to the key problem of the second commitment period: the expansion of Kyoto's Annex 1, and the establishment of a rule-based rather than ad hoc means of burden-sharing within that expanded annex.

The underlying problem is that the annexes, as currently defined, are, at best, unhelpful. By necessity, they are lists of countries that have something – but not everything – in common. They only vaguely hint at the appropriate role for each country, and they leave a great deal unsaid. Which is one of the reasons why, back in

1997, when it finally came time to allocate emission reduction targets within Annex 1, it was unclear if decisions were being made on the basis of measurable indicators of national circumstance, on the basis of political history (like those shared by the former Soviet states) or on the basis of negotiating power and acumen. It is no accident that whenever the origin of Kyoto's burden-sharing rules is at issue, discussions invariably come around to the politics of "hot air" (read "bribery") and "horse trading."

Equally confounding is the fact that today's climate negotiations take place within and between annexes as they were classified in the late 20th century, even though it is quite evident that these lists, frozen snapshots of the past, will no longer do. For, soon, the climate regime must push beyond today's Annex 1 to take account of new realities in which, for example, "newly industrialized" countries (for example, Singapore and South Korea) are far richer than many of the nations within Annex 1 (for example, the countries of eastern Europe and the former Soviet Union). Nor is this challenge of defining and updating annex membership just a near-term problem. It is a perennial challenge as countries develop and then "graduate" to assume more rigorous obligations. The problem, particularly, is that if graduation is defined as moving from one imprecisely defined annex to another, the "triggers" that signal graduation are necessarily ambiguous. And since, in almost every case, it is in the short-term interests of a country to resist graduation, this is a recipe for dysfunction. After all, if newly industrialized countries are to graduate into Annex 1, then which ones and when? And, as they say in Washington, what about China?

In 1997's Kyoto, the shortcomings of Annex I were tolerable. "Strategic ambiguity" – the watchword of the day – was good enough, and perhaps even necessary. It was fine to leave "common but differentiated" at the abstract level of preambular text. But the problems here will have to be finally faced, or at least finessed, in the post-2012 negotiations. Indeed, as the climate crisis bears down, as action becomes urgent and costs real, the stakes will only grow higher. Agreements and procedures designed to smooth and rationalize the process are needed, but, unless they are transparent, unambiguous, and based on jointly accepted principles, they will be fraught and contentious. Possibly fatally so.[51]

The most rational scheme would eliminate annexes altogether and replace them with a differentiation scheme based on a transparent, quantifiable and defensible definition of national obligation. But since such a step does not seem to be on the table, at least not yet, the question is whether Annex 1 – in the interim – can at least be rationalized and whether its membership and burden-sharing arrangements can at least be made internally consistent, and brought closer to the principles of responsibility and capacity underlying the UNFCCC. This is, in essence, what the international Climate Action Network, in its June 2007 AWG submission,[52] suggests, though only by means of a brief reference to a national "Capacity and Responsibility Indicator" that is, perhaps, too simple.[53]

Consider that problem concretely, while examining Table 4. It lists today's Annex 1 countries (in red), embedded within a larger list of the top 76 countries in the world, ranked by their "average taxpayer RCIs." That is to say, it ranks countries by their total national RCI divided by the number of people contributing to that RCI. It does this because, as we have argued, capacity and responsibility are most appropriately attributed to individuals – rich countries are not rich because of their total income, but because of their high per capita income.

These *per taxpayer* RCIs would obviously be lower – especially in developing countries – if they were calculated in *per capita* terms – dividing the national RCI by the total population rather than by the smaller number of people above the development threshold. But this would make no sense, because the people below the development threshold made no contribution to the national RCI in the first place. The key point is that the RCI is an indicator of national obligation, and national obligation should, by rights, be shared only among those above the development threshold, by those within the consuming class.

The Table 4 rankings, then, are designed to give us a sense of the relative obligations that could reasonably be assigned to a typical member of each country's consuming class. Two points are worth noting. First, this per-taxpayer obligation varies dramatically across countries. In fact, by the time we have worked our way down to the last country on the list (Belarus), it has dropped to less than one-thirtieth of that in Luxemburg, the first country on the list. Second, while today's Annex 1 countries cluster toward the top of the list, roughly a quarter of them do not even fall in the top half, while many non-Annex 1 countries do. All in all, it is plain to see that, if the current Annex 1 / non-Annex 1 distinction is going to be maintained, some countries should be added to Annex 1, and some, perhaps, should be dropped.

Table 4 also shows aggregate national RCIs, as shares of the global RCI, and cumulative RCI, as the share of the total global RCI that has been included at any point in the ranking. So, if the size of Annex 1 were to be held steady at 40 members – by dropping current members with low per-taxpayer RCI in favor of countries (now in non-Annex 1) with higher per-taxpayer RCI – the new Annex 1 would capture close to 80 percent of total global RCI. And if the membership were brought to 76 (so as to include all the countries now in Annex 1 plus any that fall between them) Annex 1 would capture almost the entire global RCI.

Rank	Country	Average "taxpayer" RCI	Percent of global RCI	Cumulative global RCI
1	Luxembourg	4111	0.08%	0.1%
2	Qatar	2741	0.09%	0.2%
3	United States	2697	34.3%	34.5%
4	Singapore	2158	0.4%	34.9%
5	Canada	2105	2.9%	37.8%
6	Australia	2103	1.8%	39.6%
7	Netherlands	2048	1.4%	41.0%
8	Norway	1975	0.4%	41.4%
9	United Arab Emirates	1912	0.4%	41.8%
10	Belgium	1862	0.8%	42.6%
11	Iceland	1847	0.02%	42.7%
12	Ireland	1845	0.3%	43.0%
13	Denmark	1820	0.4%	43.4%
14	Kuwait	1816	0.20%	43.6%
15	Finland	1679	0.4%	44.0%
16	United Kingdom	1675	4.3%	48.3%
17	Bahrain	1672	0.05%	48.3%
18	Germany	1581	5.5%	53.8%
19	Austria	1558	0.5%	54.4%
20	Japan	1504	8.1%	62.5%
21	Switzerland	1496	0.5%	63.0%
22	Taiwan	1421	1.4%	64.4%
23	Cyprus	1415	0.05%	64.4%
24	Sweden	1402	0.5%	65.0%

Rank	Country	Average "taxpayer" RCI	Percent of global RCI	Cumulative global RCI
25	France	1333	3.6%	68.5%
26	Italy	1333	3.3%	71.8%
27	New Zealand	1216	0.21%	72.0%
28	Israel	1209	0.4%	72.4%
29	Spain	1170	2.2%	74.5%
30	Greece	1097	0.5%	75.1%
31	Czech Republic	1079	0.5%	75.5%
32	Korea, Rep.	1029	2.1%	77.6%
33	Slovenia	985	0.1%	77.7%
34	Trinidad and Tobago	976	0.05%	77.8%
35	Saudi Arabia	894	0.9%	78.6%
36	Estonia	841	0.05%	78.7%
37	Portugal	819	0.4%	79.0%
38	Malta	784	0.01%	79.1%
39	Oman	712	0.08%	79.1%
40	Hungary	680	0.3%	79.4%
41	Slovak Republic	621	0.14%	79.6%
42	Poland	561	0.9%	80.5%
43	South Africa	530	1.1%	81.5%
44	Lithuania	465	0.07%	81.6%
45	Argentina	462	0.8%	82.4%
46	Libya	457	0.11%	82.5%
47	Latvia	409	0.04%	82.5%
48	Russian Federation	384	2.3%	84.8%
49	Chile	378	0.3%	85.1%
50	Malaysia	362	0.4%	85.5%
51	Croatia	355	0.07%	85.6%
52	Mexico	329	1.4%	87.0%
53	Botswana	324	0.02%	87.0%
54	Mauritius	293	0.02%	87.0%
55	Panama	240	0.03%	87.1%
56	Turkmenistan	230	0.05%	87.1%
57	Bulgaria	223	0.07%	87.2%
58	Kazakhstan	218	0.14%	87.3%
59	Romania	212	0.19%	87.5%
60	Uruguay	212	0.03%	87.5%
61	Brazil	204	1.6%	89.2%
62	Iran, Islamic Rep.	200	0.6%	89.7%
63	Namibia	196	0.02%	89.8%
64	Costa Rica	183	0.03%	89.8%
65	Thailand	178	0.5%	90.3%
66	Turkey	177	0.5%	90.8%
67	Gabon	165	0.0%	90.8%
68	Venezuela, RB	160	0.18%	91.0%
69	Dominican Republic	149	0.06%	91.1%
70	Colombia	146	0.3%	91.3%
71	Tunisia	137	0.06%	91.4%
72	China	126	7.0%	98.4%
73	Ukraine	121	0.24%	98.6%
74	Macedonia, FYR	119	0.01%	98.6%
75	Jamaica	118	0.01%	98.7%
76	Belarus	104	0.04%	98.7%

Table 4. Top 76 countries, as ranked by average "taxpayer" RCI (see text). Note that this includes all current Annex 1 countries (in red).

Unsurprisingly, and particularly if the intent is to group the countries that must take immediate hard commitments, there is no objectively correct place to draw the Annex 1 line. Any given partitioning would entail a good measure of arbitrariness. Still, if we are indeed fated to carry the Annex 1/non-Annex 1 distinction forward into the second commitment period, something like the above ranking could at least allow us to move forward into rule-based rather than ad hoc means of defining Annex 1 membership.

It could also help us to define the burden-sharing within Annex 1. A nation's portion of global RCI (column 4) is a direct indication of the portion of the global effort that it can reasonably be expected to bear, assuming, that is, that the burden-sharing arrangement aims to base obligations on responsibility and capacity. And if it does not, then this sort of ranking can tell us how far off the mark it is.

We do not, by the way, presume that this particular RCI, built up from the assumptions that we happen to find most defensible, is the last word. But for the moment, the key thing is simply to put the right pieces on the table. Which is why the RCI we have presented seeks to be consistent with a defensible definition of the right to development. That is why it is designed to measure both historical responsibility and capacity to pay, and to do so in a manner that makes sense even when comparing wealthy, middle income, and poor countries, all of which have skewed, and perhaps highly skewed, income structures. That is why it is robust enough to compare the obligations of the United States, China and Sierra Leone and produce meaningful results. These are the qualities that it must have if it is to show that a principle-based indicator need not be a mere policy abstraction, but that a proper variant, fully vetted and debated, could help to nudge the burden-sharing system forward from today's Kyoto variant, in which countries are assigned semi-arbitrary obligations within semi-arbitrary annexes, toward one that is transparently based on agreed principles. And as such, we believe it illuminates the road ahead. In any case, as Al Gore recently put it, "countries will be asked to meet different requirements based upon their historical share or contribution to the problem and their relative ability to carry the burden of change. This precedent is well established in international law, and there is no other way to do it." [54]

6.3 Last words

It is time now to act in good faith. Many years have passed since ignorance of the climate problem could honestly be cited as an excuse for inaction. The climate *problem* is now a climate *crisis*, and it is time – past time really – to admit it. Prudence no longer means modest, measured and gradual action. Indeed, the only prudent course left to us is an emergency program – one that begins immediately and takes in the whole world.

It is also time to stop pretending that the climate crisis can be solved on its own, and that the development crisis is another matter. Only a regime that structurally encompasses the right to development has any real hope of catalyzing the necessary emergency program. And hard though it may be to admit it, meaningfully recognizing the right to development inevitably means taking account of inequality within nations as well as inequality between them.

Such inequality is still a taboo subject, at least when it comes to climate policy as usual. But the longer we fear this taboo, the greater our risk of not only continued impasse, but incoherence and irrelevance as well. This is clear not only in the "What about China?" gambit that is now so popular in Washington, a gambit that presents Shanghai's affluent enclaves as if they were the whole of the Chinese nation, and thus allows the American rich to hide behind the Chinese rich. And it is clear as well in the rhetoric now popular in New Delhi, in which official climate spokesmen can confabulate India's "very, very large number of poor people" with its goal of "maintaining our current rates of GDP growth and poverty alleviation programs," and by so doing argue that, as long as India's per capita emissions remain below those of the North, its citizens (including its complement of high-emitting consumers) are in full moral compliance with their mitigation responsibilities.[55] Let us then be clear: With words like this, India matches the US gambit with another, even better one, in which India's rich can hide not only behind the North's rich, but behind India's poor as well.

The way out of this macabre dance, as we have argued, is to recognize that the right to development adheres not to nations, but to people, and that the wealthy – whether they happen to live in Washington, or Shanghai, or New Delhi – have no further claim to it at all. The alternative to this realization, and to its operationalization within a global climate regime, is to sit helplessly by as our endless negotiations, designed for a world of idealized and monolithic nations, come finally to failure, delegitimation and despair.

Which – this too must be said – is not to claim that it is the job of the climate regime to solve all the problems of the world. Inequality preceded the climate crisis, and there is little doubt that it will survive past the coming peak in global greenhouse gas emissions. But in a world as bitterly divided as ours, a viable climate regime must at least do no harm, and this means that it must not erect further barriers to the progress of the poor. The key virtue of the Greenhouse Development Rights approach is that it does not do so; indeed it is because it does not that we can claim that the GDRs approach is in fact realistic. And if the cost of meeting this condition is that, in the end, both mitigation and adaptation must be financed via a (fairly modest) tax on the luxury consumption of the relatively wealthy – for this is, finally, what GDRs proposes – well what is this but realism about our actual conditions of life on this shared, finite planet?

In the meanwhile, no one should confuse the expediency of the currently possible with the realism demanded by a true emergency program. Because if we manage to avoid a global climate catastrophe, it is not going to be by much. And the sooner the architecture of the climate regime is aligned to the real structure of the problem, the better our chances are going to be.

Concentrating solar power: a huge source for clean power generation in desert regions

7 Technical Appendices

7.1 Appendix A: The GDRs database

The database used in the Greenhouse Development Rights paper (hereafter "the GDRs database") has been assembled from a variety of publicly available data sources, with some missing elements calculated on the basis of other elements, and some missing elements (for example, Gini coefficients for some countries) filled in with educated guesses.

The GDRs database includes 158 countries accounting for about 99.7 percent of the world population in 2005, according to the World Bank's *World Development Indicators* online database (hereafter WDI). Most of the excluded countries are small island states, including some that are members of the UNFCCC. *

The key elements in the GDRs database, from which all the calculations are derived, are the following:

- Population in 2005
- Per capita income (PPP adjusted) in 2005 (in turn derived from GNP and population)
- Gini coefficient
- Cumulative per capita CO_2 emissions from fossil fuels (and cement), 1990–2005

The reasons for limiting the emissions database to only CO_2, and excluding CO_2 from land-use change, are both technical and political, and are discussed briefly in Section 3 of the main text. We expect there to be much further discussion of these issues. Similarly, the use of per capita income as an indicator of "capacity" or development status is not intended to preclude alternative formulations.

* The included countries – not all of them UNFCCC members – are shown in Table A1 below; the excluded countries that are UNFCCC members are Antigua and Barbuda, the Bahamas, Belize, Bhutan, Cape Verde, Comoros, Cook Islands, Djibouti, Dominica, Fiji, Grenada, Kiribati, Liechtenstein, Maldives, Marshall Islands, Micronesia, Monaco, Nauru, Niue, St. Kitts and Nevis, St. Vincent and the Grenadines, Samoa, San Marino, Sao Tome and Principe, Seychelles, the Solomon Islands, Suriname, Timor-leste, Tonga, Tuvalu and Vanuatu. UNFCCC observers Andorra, Brunei and the Holy See are also excluded, as is the West Bank and Gaza Strip.

7.1.1 Data sources *

Population

The population data for 2005 is taken from the World Bank's WDI, with the exception of four countries: Serbia, Afghanistan, Iraq and Taiwan.** For Serbia, a 2005 regional survey reported in Wikipedia was used; for the other three, 2007 population estimates were taken from the CIA World Factbook, and back-dated to 2005 by subtracting two years of population growth at the estimated 2007 population growth rate. For countries with territories that are included separately in the EIA and WDI databases (i.e., China, the United States, Denmark, the Netherlands, France, and the United Kingdom), available information for the territories was aggregated from the WDI database or alternate sources (the CIA Factbook or Wikipedia) into a single population figure for the country (see Table A1 for details).

Per capita income

Income data (gross domestic product for 2005, purchasing power parity adjusted, current [2005] international dollars) is taken from the WDI, except for 15 countries (see Table A1), for which data was taken from the CIA Factbook and adjusted to 2005 by forward or backward extrapolation with estimated growth rates. GDP was divided by the population in 2005 to generate per capita income in 2005. For countries with territories reported separately in the WDI database, the GNP and population figures from those territories were also aggregated into the countries' per capita income.

Gini coefficient

Gini coefficients were taken from the World Income Inequality Database (WIID v. 2.0b, http://www.wider.unu.edu/wiid/wiid.htm) for all but about 30 countries. The national values were selected by first filtering to ensure that only data was used that covered the entire geographic extent of a country and all of its population, then selecting the most suitable based on the date of the data (with the most recent year preferred) and the quality of the data as reported in the WIID database. In a few of the other cases, where Gini coefficients were not in the WIID database, published Gini coefficients were available from other sources (for example, the EU's Europa database for Malta and Cyprus). For the remainder, Ginis were estimated on the basis of comparable countries. These countries (indicated in Table A1) include only about 6 percent of the global population and are generally (though not exclusively) smaller and poorer countries, so any disagreement between the estimated and true values should not greatly affect the calculated global RCI and thus the national RCIs for countries which

---

* Note that this methodology and the resulting database and calculations differs very slightly from that used in the original electronically published version dated September 24, 2007. This is due primarily to the availability of 2005 data from the USEIA, as well as some additional changes and corrections discussed in the next section.

** Note that Taiwan is not a member of the UN, and thus cannot join the UNFCCC. This raises interesting and rarely discussed issues, given that it is roughly the world's 14th largest economy, ranked 22nd per capita by our responsibility and capacity indicator, and accounts for over 1 percent of global emissions.

have published Gini coefficients. Note also that the measurement of Gini coefficients is in general only approximate, and in countries undergoing rapid economic changes they can change significantly over even a fairly small number of years. Though they are a useful and widely cited indicator of income distribution, refinements are an important subject for further research.

Cumulative per capita emissions from fossil fuels, 1990–2005

The emissions component of the GDRs database was compiled from two primary sources: the US Department of Energy's Energy Information Administration (EIA)* and the World Resources Institute's Climate Analysis Indicators Tool (CAIT).**

A full 1990–2005 dataset was available from the US EIA for most of our 158 countries, with the exception of Eritrea and the countries that were part of the former USSR, the former Yugoslavia, and the former Czechoslovakia, which were typically missing the data for 1990 and 1991. The CAIT database has estimated the fraction of emissions of the pre-independence countries attributable to these now-independent nations. Thus to calculate a full estimate of cumulative emissions, data for the years missing from the EIA database were taken from the CAIT database and were added to the annual estimates from the US EIA database.***

The EIA database includes as separate listings many geographic entities that are part of the same country in the UNFCCC regime; for example, China, Hong Kong and Macau are all included separately, as are the United States, Puerto Rico and various other territories of the United States. The territories included in the aggregate emissions figure for the five countries with territories listed separately are given in the footnotes to Table A1 below.

Annual emissions for the years 1990–2005 in MtC were added to get cumulative emissions, and then divided by population in 2005 to get "cumulative emissions per capita." Obviously one could account for changing population over time as well, but the results would likely not vary by much.

7.1.2 Master data table

The four primary variables used in the GDRs calculations are shown below for all 158 countries, along with their classification as Annex I, EITs (Economies in Transition), LDCs (Least Developed Countries), and "European Union Era." This latter is coded as 1 for EU 15, 2 for EU 25, and 3 for EU 27. Aggregated data for the EU is for the EU 27, unless specified otherwise. Income class is per the World Bank's classification (see note 33 to the main text). For a machine-readable copy of this data, please contact GDRs@ecoequity.org or visit gdrs.sourceforge.net.

* US Energy Information Adminstration, *International Energy Annual 2005*, Table H.1co2, available online at http://www.eia.doe.gov/iea/. Table dated Sept. 18, 2007.

** Climate Analysis Indicators Tool (CAIT) version 4.0. (Washington, DC: World Resources Institute, 2007). Available at http://cait.wri.org.

*** Although it does not say so anywhere that we were able to find, the US EIA database appears to include international bunker fuels; thus to fill in the missing years we also used the CAIT figures with international bunker fuels.

Table A1. Master data table. Country names in italics are those for which income data came from the CIA Factbook rather than the World Bank, per above. Gini coefficients that are underlined are educated guesses.

Country	Per capita income 2005 ($ PPP)	Pop 2005	Gini latest	Cumulative per capita CO_2 1990–2005	Annex 1	EIT	LDC	EU Era	Income class
Afghanistan	654	30,255,865	50.0	0.2	0	0	1	0	Low
Albania	5,318	3,129,678	28.1	4.8	0	1	0	0	Lower Middle
Algeria	7,062	32,853,798	35.4	11.0	0	0	0	0	Lower Middle
Angola	2,335	15,941,392	50.0	3.5	0	0	1	0	Lower Middle
Argentina	14,286	38,747,148	50.0	14.2	0	0	0	0	Upper Middle
Armenia	4,952	3,016,312	47.4	11.7	0	1	0	0	Lower Middle
Australia	33,993	20,329,000	29.3	69.7	1	0	0	0	High
Austria	33,537	8,233,300	26.0	34.1	1	0	0	1	High
Azerbaijan	5,027	8,388,000	37.3	22.4	0	1	0	0	Lower Middle
Bahrain	21,491	726,617	50.0	111.7	0	0	0	0	High
Bangladesh	2,054	141,822,276	31.7	0.8	0	0	1	0	Low
Belarus	7,922	9,775,591	23.8	30.7	1	1	0	0	Lower Middle
Belgium	32,702	10,478,650	26.0	56.5	1	0	0	1	High
Benin	1,130	8,438,853	36.0	0.7	0	0	1	0	Low
Bolivia	2,820	9,182,015	60.1	3.9	0	0	0	0	Lower Middle
Bosnia and Herzegovina	6,074	3,907,074	26.0	15.7	0	1	0	0	Lower Middle
Botswana	12,154	1,764,926	53.7	8.5	0	0	0	0	Upper Middle
Brazil	8,587	186,404,913	56.6	7.1	0	0	0	0	Lower Middle
Bulgaria	9,226	7,740,000	32.2	29.6	1	1	0	3	Lower Middle
Burkina Faso	1,249	13,227,835	62.5	0.3	0	0	1	0	Low
Burundi	699	7,547,515	41.8	0.2	0	0	1	0	Low
Cambodia	2,727	14,071,014	44.5	0.2	0	0	1	0	Low
Cameroon	2,300	16,321,863	44.0	1.6	0	0	0	0	Lower Middle
Canada	33,370	32,299,000	30.1	73.0	1	0	0	0	High
Central African Republic	1,224	4,037,747	64.9	0.3	0	0	1	0	Low
Chad	1,524	9,748,931	50.0	0.1	0	0	1	0	Low
Chile	11,940	16,295,102	54.6	12.8	0	0	0	0	Upper Middle
China*	6,920	1,311,903,762	44.9	10.7	0	0	0	0	Lower Middle
Colombia	7,346	44,945,790	56.2	5.4	0	0	0	0	Lower Middle
Congo, Dem. Rep.	716	57,548,744	50.0	0.2	0	0	0	0	Low
Congo, Rep.	1,257	3,998,904	50.0	3.2	0	0	0	0	Lower Middle
Costa Rica	10,192	4,327,228	47.9	4.6	0	0	0	0	Upper Middle
Cote d'Ivoire	1,616	18,153,867	44.5	1.3	0	0	0	0	Low
Croatia	13,055	4,443,350	29.0	18.9	1	1	0	4	Upper Middle
Cuba	3,645	11,269,400	25.0	12.4	0	0	0	0	Lower Middle
Cyprus	28,372	757,800	27.0	40.8	0	0	0	2	High
Czech Republic	20,845	10,234,092	22.8	51.7	1	1	0	2	Upper Middle
Denmark**	34,030	5,521,213	24.0	48.5	1	0	0	1	High
Dominican Republic	7,854	9,469,601	50.6	6.2	0	0	0	0	Lower Middle
Ecuador	4,342	13,228,423	58.8	6.5	0	0	0	0	Lower Middle
Egypt, Arab Rep.	4,321	74,032,884	37.8	6.8	0	0	0	0	Lower Middle
El Salvador	5,255	6,880,951	48.4	3.0	0	0	0	0	Lower Middle
Eritrea	1,109	4,401,357	50.0	0.8	0	0	0	0	Low
Estonia	15,968	1,346,100	35.5	61.8	1	1	0	2	Upper Middle
Ethiopia	1,084	71,256,000	29.5	0.2	0	0	0	0	Low
Finland	32,466	5,246,100	25.0	44.4	1	0	0	1	High
France***	31,155	63,160,207	28.0	27.6	1	0	0	1	High
Gabon	6,585	1,383,841	50.0	17.0	0	0	0	0	Upper Middle
Gambia, The	1,921	1,517,079	47.1	0.7	0	0	0	0	Low

* Includes Hong Kong and Macao.

** Includes Greenland and the Faroe Islands.

*** Includes French Guiana, French Polynesia, Guadelupe, Martinique, La Reunion, New Caledonia, St. Pierre and Miquilon.

Country	Per capita income 2005 ($ PPP)	Pop 2005	Gini latest	Cumulative per capita CO_2 1990–2005	Annex 1	EIT	LDC	EU Era	Income class
Georgia	3,366	4,474,404	36.7	6.8	0	1	0	0	Lower Middle
Germany	29,980	82,469,400	31.1	46.5	1	0	0	1	High
Ghana	2,480	22,112,805	40.7	0.9	0	0	0	0	Low
Greece	23,377	11,104,000	33.0	36.3	1	0	0	1	High
Guatemala	4,568	12,599,059	49.4	2.6	0	0	0	0	Lower Middle
Guinea	2,350	9,002,656	55.1	0.6	0	0	0	0	Low
Guinea-Bissau	827	1,586,344	44.3	0.9	0	0	0	0	Low
Guyana	4,508	751,218	44.2	7.5	0	0	0	0	Lower Middle
Haiti	1,648	8,527,777	50.9	0.6	0	0	0	0	Low
Honduras	3,430	7,204,723	54.5	2.6	0	0	0	0	Lower Middle
Hungary	18,256	10,087,050	25.2	25.6	1	1	0	2	Upper Middle
Iceland	37,096	296,750	30.0	41.0	1	0	0	0	High
India	3,452	1,094,583,000	36.0	3.5	0	0	0	0	Low
Indonesia	3,847	220,558,000	33.9	4.9	0	0	0	0	Lower Middle
Iran, Islamic Rep.	7,971	68,251,085	44.0	19.2	0	0	0	0	Lower Middle
Iraq	3,304	26,096,804	41.5	12.1	0	0	0	0	Lower Middle
Ireland	38,892	4,159,100	32.0	36.8	1	0	0	1	High
Israel	25,875	6,923,600	37.2	34.2	0	0	0	0	High
Italy	29,209	58,607,050	33.0	32.2	1	0	0	1	High
Jamaica	4,293	2,654,500	59.9	16.5	0	0	0	0	Lower Middle
Japan	30,736	127,774,000	31.9	38.5	1	0	0	0	High
Jordan	5,593	5,411,500	36.4	11.4	0	0	0	0	Lower Middle
Kazakhstan	7,860	15,147,050	35.9	49.7	0	1	0	0	Lower Middle
Kenya	1,240	34,255,722	55.6	1.0	0	0	0	0	Low
Korea, Dem. Rep.	1,750	22,487,661	40.0	15.7	0	0	0	0	Low
Korea, Rep.	22,080	48,294,143	36.9	35.6	0	0	0	0	High
Kuwait	26,321	2,535,446	45.0	86.1	0	0	0	0	High
Kyrgyz Republic	1,936	5,143,500	35.2	6.6	0	1	0	0	Low
Lao PDR	2,139	5,663,910	36.5	0.5	0	0	0	0	Low
Latvia	13,700	2,300,500	35.9	17.8	1	1	0	2	Upper Middle
Lebanon	5,542	4,010,740	45.0	14.3	0	0	0	0	Upper Middle
Lesotho	3,384	1,794,769	60.0	0.4	0	0	0	0	Lower Middle
Liberia	786	3,283,267	50.0	0.6	0	0	0	0	Low
Libya	11,635	5,853,452	45.0	31.8	0	0	0	0	Upper Middle
Lithuania	14,584	3,414,300	32.4	21.1	1	1	0	2	Upper Middle
Luxembourg	64,088	456,710	26.0	97.5	1	0	0	0	High
Macedonia, FYR	7,189	2,034,060	35.2	19.5	0	1	0	0	Lower Middle
Madagascar	924	18,605,921	47.4	0.4	0	0	0	0	Low
Malawi	669	12,883,935	49.3	0.2	0	0	0	0	Low
Malaysia	10,887	25,347,368	49.9	18.4	0	0	0	0	Upper Middle
Mali	1,034	13,518,416	54.0	0.2	0	0	0	0	Low
Malta	19,197	403,500	30.0	29.6	0	0	0	2	High
Mauritania	2,234	3,068,742	39.0	4.1	0	0	1	0	Low
Mauritius	12,720	1,243,253	37.1	10.0	0	0	0	0	Upper Middle
Mexico	10,811	103,089,133	49.9	14.8	0	0	0	0	Upper Middle
Moldova	2,298	3,876,661	43.6	11.5	0	1	0	0	Lower Middle
Mongolia	2,135	2,554,000	44.0	13.8	0	0	0	0	Low
Morocco	4,608	30,142,709	39.0	4.2	0	0	0	0	Lower Middle
Mozambique	1,226	19,792,295	39.4	0.3	0	0	1	0	Low
Myanmar	1,636	50,519,492	50.0	0.7	0	0	1	0	Low
Namibia	7,634	2,031,252	73.9	3.8	0	0	0	0	Lower Middle
Nepal	1,551	27,132,629	46.7	0.3	0	0	1	0	Low
Netherlands*	33,871	16,602,806	27.0	65.8	1	0	0	1	High
New Zealand	25,706	4,098,900	34.1	35.8	1	0	0	0	High
Nicaragua	3,911	5,149,311	54.4	2.7	0	0	0	0	Lower Middle
Niger	786	13,956,977	50.6	0.4	0	0	1	0	Low
Nigeria	1,095	141,356,083	50.2	2.8	0	0	0	0	Low
Norway	41,327	4,623,300	25.0	38.1	1	0	0	1	High

* Includes the Netherlands Antilles and Aruba.

Country	Per capita income 2005 ($ PPP)	Pop 2005	Gini latest	Cumulative per capita CO_2 1990-2005	Annex 1	EIT	LDC	EU Era	Income class
Oman	16,191	2,566,981	45.0	32.0	0	0	0	0	Upper Middle
Pakistan	2,383	155,772,000	31.0	2.6	0	0	0	0	Low
Panama	7,644	3,231,502	54.8	17.4	0	0	0	0	Upper Middle
Papua New Guinea	2,563	5,887,138	50.4	2.2	0	0	0	0	Low
Paraguay	4,819	5,898,651	55.2	2.3	0	0	0	0	Lower Middle
Peru	6,042	27,968,244	52.0	3.9	0	0	0	0	Lower Middle
Philippines	5,140	83,054,478	47.9	3.2	0	0	0	0	Lower Middle
Poland	14,167	38,165,450	35.2	35.3	1	1	0	2	Upper Middle
Portugal	21,125	10,549,450	38.0	22.6	1	0	0	1	High
Qatar	30,173	812,842	50.0	167.6	0	0	0	0	High
Romania	9,064	21,634,350	35.2	23.0	1	1	0	3	Upper Middle
Russian Federation	10,846	143,113,650	31.0	52.3	1	1	0	0	Upper Middle
Rwanda	1,206	9,037,690	45.4	0.4	0	0	1	0	Low
Saudi Arabia	16,601	23,118,994	45.0	52.3	0	0	0	0	High
Senegal	1,780	11,658,172	29.3	1.4	0	0	1	0	Low
Serbia*	5,666	7,440,769	24.0	26.4	0	1	0	0	Lower Middle
Sierra Leone	806	5,525,478	39.0	0.7	0	0	1	0	Low
Singapore	29,842	4,341,800	48.1	95.7	0	0	0	0	High
Slovak Republic	15,991	5,387,000	25.5	34.1	1	1	0	2	Upper Middle
Slovenia	22,282	2,000,500	22.1	33.2	1	1	0	2	High
Somalia	627	8,227,826	47.4	0.3	0	0	1	0	Low
South Africa	11,187	46,888,200	56.5	33.8	0	0	0	0	Upper Middle
Spain	26,792	43,398,150	31.0	29.4	1	0	0	1	High
Sri Lanka	4,632	19,625,384	27.6	2.0	0	0	0	0	Lower Middle
St. Lucia	6,997	164,791	43.0	6.6	0	0	0	0	Upper Middle
Sudan	2,083	36,232,945	50.0	0.7	0	0	1	0	Low
Swaziland	4,868	1,131,000	59.2	3.7	0	0	0	0	Lower Middle
Sweden	32,801	9,024,040	23.0	27.6	1	0	0	1	High
Switzerland	35,893	7,437,100	31.1	26.1	1	0	0	0	High
Syrian Arab Republic	3,832	19,043,382	45.0	10.2	0	0	0	0	Lower Middle
Taiwan	28,606	22,720,312	33.9	39.9	0	0	0	0	High
Tajikistan	1,338	6,550,213	32.5	4.5	0	1	0	0	Low
Tanzania	707	38,477,873	36.7	0.3	0	0	1	0	Low
Thailand	8,701	64,232,758	42.7	10.7	0	0	0	0	Lower Middle
Togo	1,483	6,145,004	50.0	0.8	0	0	1	0	Low
Trinidad and Tobago	14,735	1,305,236	49.3	85.0	0	0	0	0	Upper Middle
Tunisia	8,375	10,029,000	40.6	7.6	0	0	0	0	Lower Middle
Turkey	8,408	72,065,000	45.0	10.5	1	0	0	4	Upper Middle
Turkmenistan	8,324	4,833,266	42.1	26.0	0	1	0	0	Lower Middle
Uganda	1,454	28,816,229	46.9	0.2	0	0	1	0	Low
Ukraine	6,858	47,075,295	32.7	37.8	1	1	0	0	Lower Middle
United Arab Emirates	25,514	4,533,145	45.0	106.0	0	0	0	0	High
United Kingdom**	33,175	60,418,273	35.0	41.5	1	0	0	1	High
United States***	41,565	300,659,101	46.4	80.4	1	0	0	0	High
Uruguay	10,419	3,305,723	45.0	7.0	0	0	0	0	Upper Middle
Uzbekistan	2,064	26,167,369	48.1	18.7	0	1	0	0	Low
Venezuela, RB	6,717	26,577,000	45.4	21.3	0	0	0	0	Upper Middle
Vietnam	3,076	83,104,900	36.8	2.2	0	0	0	0	Low
Yemen, Rep.	962	20,974,655	21.8	2.4	0	0	1	0	Low
Zambia	1,023	11,668,457	57.4	0.8	0	0	1	0	Low
Zimbabwe	2,065	13,009,534	73.3	4.6	0	0	0	0	Low

* Published data for Serbia and Montenegro (the latter of which became independent in 2006) were multiplied by 0.93 to estimate the data for Serbia alone, based on population fraction.

** Includes the British Virgin Islands, Gibraltar, Bermuda, Cayman Islands, Falkland Islands, Montserrat, Saint Helena, Turks and Caicos Islands.

*** Includes Puerto Rico, Guam, the US Virgin Islands and American Samoa.

7.2 Appendix B: GDRs calculations

7.2.1 Overview of GDRs calculations architecture

The heart of the GDRs analysis is the estimation of the capacity and responsibility of each country, and thus the Responsibility and Capacity Indicator (RCI), as per the definitions in the main text. This calculation requires four data elements for each country (population, per capita income, per capita cumulative emissions and Gini coefficient). The definitions and sources we use for these data elements are given in Appendix A.

In addition to data for each country, the RCI calculation depends on the specification of a development threshold, above which a person's income contributes to the calculation of capacity, and which is also used to calculate the portion of a person's emissions that contributes to the calculation of responsibility. The development threshold used was $9,000, PPP adjusted; the justification for this figure is given in Section 3 of the main text. This calculation also requires an assumption about distribution of income and emissions within a country, for which we describe our approximation below.

The GDRs database is maintained in Excel, while the calculation of the RCI is done by a script written in the Tcl/Tk language using a data file created from the Excel database. Output from the script was imported back into Excel to produce the various tables and graphs. Additional calculations of emissions, population and income projections (used in Section 5) are done in a model built in the Stella modeling language. The software and data are available at http://gdrs.sourceforge.net.

7.2.2 Calculation formulas

Conceptually, the calculation of responsibility and capacity is based on the assumption that the distribution of income across individuals in a country can be approximated by a log-normal income distribution. We also assume that within a given country, the distribution of emissions is proportional to consumption, which is in turn proportional to income. With these two assumptions, it is possible to use relatively simple analytical formulas and functions to calculate the RCI for each country by aggregating RCI across individuals by means of a simple integration across the full income range (done numerically in Tcl/Tk programming language).

The log-normal model of income distribution

The calculations used in this paper are based on the approximation that income distribution can be modeled reasonably well as a continuous log-normal distribution, which requires the specification of only two parameters: the country's per capita income, and its Gini coefficient, a well-known measure of inequality.

A graph of the log-normal distribution is shown in Figure A1 below, for two hypothetical countries with the same per capita income ($15,000 per capita) and Gini coefficients of 0.3 (dotted line) and 0.5 (solid line). The measure on the y-axis is a metric called the "probability density," which shows the relative number of people at each income level.

The log-normal distribution is defined as a distribution that is normal (the classic, symmetrical bell-curve shape) in the natural logarithm* of the variable of interest. There are, in this case, two important features of the log-normal distribution: First, none of it is below zero (essential for a measure of income distribution); and second, it has a very long "tail" on the right. As a model of income distribution, this means that most of the population will have incomes near the modal (most common) value (the peak), which is slightly lower than the mean (average) per capita income, but that a significant fraction will have higher incomes, and a small fraction will have incomes many times the mean per capita income.

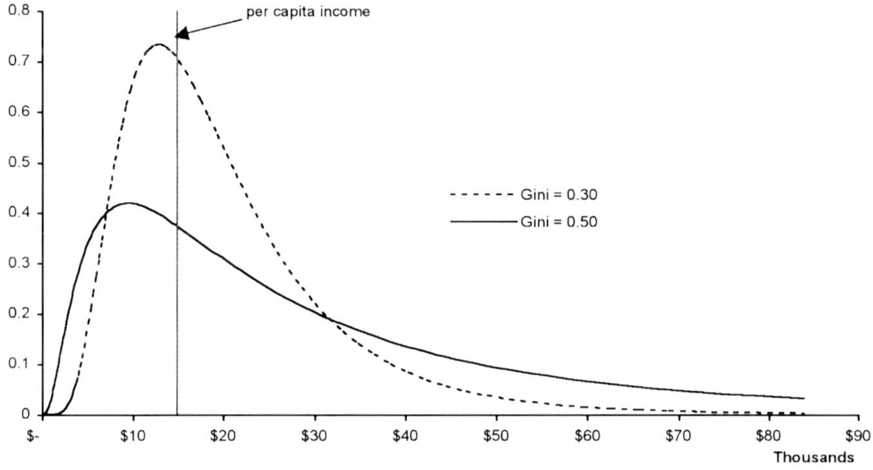

Figure A1. The log-normal distribution as a model of income distribution for two hypothetical countries with per capita income of $15,000, with Gini coefficients of 0.30 and 0.50 respectively.

The log-normal distribution has been proposed as an adequate model of income distribution since at least the work of Cowell (1995). A detailed discussion of the justification and some alternatives is available in Kemp-Benedict (2001). A more recent defense, based on a new statistical analysis, was offered by Humberto Lopez and Servén (2006) of the World Bank.

Using the log-normal distribution to calculate the RCI

As noted above, the RCI is calculated using scripts written in the Tcl/Tk language. The scripts and a Windows executable "RCI calculator" based on them are available from http://gdrs.sourceforge.net/. Because of the assumption that both income distribution and the distribution of emissions can be modeled by the log-normal distribution, analytical solutions exist for the calculations of R, C and the RCI, that are at the core of calculation. These are presented immediately below. Those not interested in the derivation of these integral solutions might choose to skip this section, going instead

* You do not need to understand logarithms to follow the calculations. However, if you are not familiar with logarithms and want to learn more about them, there are several web-based tutorials available, such as "What on Earth is a Logarithm," by Peter Alfeld of the University of Utah (http://www.math.utah.edu/~pa/math/log.html).

to the following section, which presents a more graphically intuitive explanation of the calculations.

Integral solutions for R, C and RCI

For national capacity, we have by definition

$$C = P \int_{y_{DT}}^{\infty} dy \ (y - y_{DT}) f(y, \bar{y}, G) \tag{1}$$

where, P is the population, y_{DT} is the development threshold, $\bar{y}$ is the per capita income, G is the Gini coefficient, and the log-normal income distribution $f(y, \bar{y}, G)$ is given by

$$f(y, \bar{y}, G) = \frac{1}{\sqrt{2\pi\sigma^2(G)}} \exp\left[-\frac{1}{2\sigma^2(G)} \left(\ln\frac{y}{\bar{y}} + \frac{\sigma^2(G)}{2} \right)^2 \right] \tag{2a}$$

where the dependence on the Gini coefficient is fully contained in the variance

$$\sigma^2(G) = 2\left[N^{-1}\left(\frac{1+G}{2} \right) \right]^2 \tag{2b}$$

and N^{-1} is the inverse of the cumulative normal distribution.

For national responsibility, we have

$$R = P \int_{y_{DT}}^{\infty} dy \left(e(y) - e_{DT}\right) f(y, \bar{y}, G) \tag{3a}$$

where e is emissions at a given level of income, and e_{DT} is equal to the emissions of a person whose income is precisely equal to the development threshold. The quantity e_{DT} behaves analogously to the development threshold, as the "emission threshold," such that only emissions above this threshold contribute to R. The assumption that emissions are proportional to income allows us to reexpress equation (3a) using the proportionality constant $(E / \bar{y})$, where E is the average per capita historical emissions. Expressing e_{DT} as $(E/\bar{y}) \cdot y_{DT}$, we have

$$R = P \int_{y_{DT}}^{\infty} dy \ \frac{E}{\bar{y}} (y - y_{DT}) f(y, \bar{y}, G) \tag{3b}$$

Since f $(y, \bar{y}, G)$ is the log-normal distribution, both R and C can now be calculated (making use of the known expression for the first moment of the cumulative log-normal distribution) as

$$C = P \times \left\{ \bar{y}\left\{ 1 - N\left[\frac{1}{\sigma(G)} \left(\ln\frac{y_{DT}}{\bar{y}} - \frac{\sigma^2(G)}{2} \right) \right] \right\} - y_{DT}\left\{ 1 - N\left[\frac{1}{\sigma(G)} \left(\ln\frac{y_{DT}}{\bar{y}} + \frac{\sigma^2(G)}{2} \right) \right] \right\} \right\} \tag{4a}$$

and

$$R = P\frac{E}{\bar{y}} \times \left\{ \bar{y}\left\{1 - N\left[\frac{1}{\sigma(G)}\left(\ln\frac{y_{DT}}{\bar{y}} - \frac{\sigma^2(G)}{2}\right)\right]\right\} - y_{DT}\left\{1 - N\left[\frac{1}{\sigma(G)}\left(\ln\frac{y_{DT}}{\bar{y}} + \frac{\sigma^2(G)}{2}\right)\right]\right\}\right\} \quad (4b)$$

To calculate national RCI, we start with the definition, RCI = $R^a C^b$ for each individual and we integrate over the entire income distribution

$$\mathrm{RCI} = \int_{y_{DT}}^{\infty} dy\, R(y)^a\, C(y)^b\, f(y,\bar{y},G) \quad (5a)$$

and, thus

$$\mathrm{RCI} = \int_{y_{DT}}^{\infty} dy\,(y - y_{DT})^a \left[\frac{E}{\bar{y}}(y - y_{DT})\right]^b f(y,\bar{y},G) \quad (5b)$$

This can be rearranged to give

$$\mathrm{RCI} = \left(\frac{E}{\bar{y}}\right)^b \int_{y_{DT}}^{\infty} dy\,(y - y_{DT})^{a+b} f(y,\bar{y},G) \quad (5c)$$

Since a and b are weightings, they satisfy $a + b = 1$ by definition. This ensures that the definition RCI = $R^a C^b$ adheres to the intuitive property that a 1 percent increase in R will raise RCI by a percent, a 1 percent increase in R will raise RCI by b percent, and a 1 percent increase in both R and C will raise RCI by 1 percent. Equation (5c) thus becomes

$$\mathrm{RCI} = \left(\frac{E}{\bar{y}}\right)^b \int_{y_{DT}}^{\infty} dy\,(y - y_{DT}) f(y,\bar{y},G) \quad (5d)$$

Again because $a + b = 1$, this can be written

$$\mathrm{RCI} = \left[\int_{y_{DT}}^{\infty} dy\,(y - y_{DT}) f(y,\bar{y},G)\right]^a \left[\left(\frac{E}{\bar{y}}\right)\int_{y_{DT}}^{\infty} dy\,(y - y_{DT}) f(y,\bar{y},G)\right]^b \quad (5d)$$

The two integrals in square brackets are precisely the definitions of the national capacity, C, and national responsibility, R, so we have

$$\mathrm{RCI} = C^a\ R^b \quad (5e)$$

at the national level as well as the individual level, allowing us to calculate the national RCI from the national R and C calculated as per equations (4a) and (4b).

Graphical explanations for R, C and RCI

The same calculation can be described in more graphical terms, referring to Figure A1. (Keep in mind that the shape of the curve will be different for countries with different per capita incomes and different Gini coefficients.)

The x-axis, which measures income, can be divided into arbitrarily small sections – call them "bins" – for example, exactly one dollar wide. For a country with a given population, there will be a specific number of people in each bin, proportional to the height of the income distribution curve on the y-axis at the particular income value on the x-axis.

Given our assumption that emissions in a given country are distributed proportionally to income, we can also calculate the emissions associated with the people in each bin. Straightforwardly, since a person with the average (per capita) income also has the average (per capita) emissions, the emissions for a person at any other income value is simply equal to the average per capita emissions times the ratio of that person's income to the average per capita income, which is expressed above as $(E/\bar{y})$. The assumption that emissions are proportional to income implies that the Gini coefficient affects the distribution of emissions in precisely the same manner as income.

To calculate the RCI, given the values for income and emissions in each bin, we need first to calculate the portion of each exceeding the development threshold and the associated "emissions threshold." That is, capacity C of a person in this bin is given by $C = y - y_{DT}$, where as before y is income and y_{DT} is the development threshold, and so, for persons with income of \$15,000 and our development threshold of \$9,000, then C = \$6,000. Similarly, $R = e - e_{DT}$, where e equals emissions, and e_{DT} serves as an emissions threshold (as above), given by the emissions of someone whose income is precisely equal to the development threshold; say, hypothetically, 9 tC cumulatively between 1990 and 2005. Then for a person with an income of \$15,000, their responsibility R would be (15,000/9,000) × 9 – 9 = 6. Then using the definition of the RCI, which is C^aR^b, with $a = 0.4$ and $b = 0.6$, we get for this typical individual in the bin RCI = $6{,}000^{0.6}$ x $6^{0.4}$ = 379. By comparison, for a person with an income of \$20,000, their contribution to their country's RCI would be $(20{,}0000 - 9{,}000)^{0.6}$ $(20{,}000/6{,}000) * 9 - 9)^{0.4}$ = 694. The resulting number is measured in units of dollars^a ·tonnes^b, and can be compared across countries. Note, relative RCI (for example, national RCI as a fraction of global RCI) can be compared for different values of the weightings a and b, but absolute values cannot since they are measured in different units.

Finally, to calculate the national RCI, multiply the RCI for a typical person in each bin by the number of people in that bin, then sum the values for each bin, up to an income level sufficiently high to capture the entire population. Thus, given specific choice of development threshold and the weighting exponents, every person, and thus every country, has a well-defined RCI, and their share of the global total can be calculated.

7.2.3 Output table for all countries

The central calculation made for each country is a single responsibility/capacity indicator (we call it an indicator rather than an index because it measures a "quantity," rather than being a comparison of one country to another). In principle the RCI for two hypothetical individuals in different countries who have the same income and historical emissions contribute the same amount to their country's (and thus the world's) RCI; thus countries with the same per capita income, cumulative per capita emissions and Gini coefficient, but with different populations, would have different national RCIs, exactly proportional to their populations, but identical per capita RCIs and thus identical per capita obligations. (Note that in the context of a cap-and-allocate model (per chapter 5), such countries could still have different allocations if they had different "no regrets" baselines.)

Table A2 below shows the RCI calculations for the 158 countries in our primary database and 11 aggregated regions, using our default assumptions (i.e., a development threshold of $9,000 PPP adjusted, cumulative per capita CO_2 emissions from fossil fuel consumption 1990–2005, per capita income in 2005 [PPP adjusted] and capacity weighted slightly more than responsibility [see above]). The table shows for each country its share of global population, its calculated capacity as a percentage of GDP, its national share of the total global RCI, the fraction of the population above the development threshold, the RCI per capita for the fraction of the population above the development threshold, and its rank in order of average "taxpayer" RCI. (See the discussion in the main text regarding the average "taxpayer" RCI.)

Table A2. RCI calculations for all countries and country groups.

Country or region	Share of global population (percent)	Percentage of population above the cutoff	Capacity (percent of GDP)	Share of global RCI (percent)	Average "taxpayer" RCI	Rank by average "taxpayer" RCI
Afghanistan	0.47	0.1	0.3	0.0	0	146
Albania	0.05	9.9	5.1	0.0	16	102
Algeria	0.51	24.3	17.2	0.1	91	79
Angola	0.25	2.9	6.1	0.0	11	105
Argentina	0.6	50.3	51.5	0.8	462	45
Armenia	0.05	13.3	17.3	0.0	76	82
Australia	0.32	98.7	73.6	1.8	2103	6
Austria	0.13	99.5	73.2	0.5	1558	19
Azerbaijan	0.13	11.7	9.8	0.0	57	84
Bahrain	0.01	66.8	63.8	0.1	1672	17
Bangladesh	2.2	0.2	0.2	0.0	0	144
Belarus	0.15	30.4	12.1	0.0	104	76
Belgium	0.16	99.4	72.5	0.8	1862	10
Benin	0.13	0.0	0.0	0.0	0	153
Bolivia	0.14	5.8	16.7	0.0	34	95
Bosnia and Herzegovina	0.06	14.2	6.3	0.0	35	94
Botswana	0.03	40.9	48.8	0.0	324	53
Brazil	2.9	27.6	40.7	1.6	204	61
Bulgaria	0.12	40.1	24.1	0.1	223	57
Burkina Faso	0.21	1.4	7.2	0.0	3	117
Burundi	0.12	0.0	0.0	0.0	0	154
Cambodia	0.22	3.2	4.9	0.0	3	118
Cameroon	0.25	1.9	3.1	0.0	4	116
Canada	0.5	98.3	73.1	2.9	2105	5
Central African Republic	0.06	1.5	8.7	0.0	4	115
Chad	0.15	1.0	2.6	0.0	1	133
Chile	0.25	39.7	48.8	0.3	378	49
China	20.39	23.2	24.3	7.0	126	72
Colombia	0.7	23.2	35.8	0.3	146	70
Congo, Dem. Rep.	0.89	0.1	0.4	0.0	0	145
Congo, Rep.	0.06	0.6	1.7	0.0	2	127
Costa Rica	0.07	37.5	39.1	0.0	183	64
Cote d'Ivoire	0.28	0.7	1.4	0.0	1	130
Croatia	0.07	67.2	37.1	0.1	355	51
Cuba	0.18	1.3	0.6	0.0	2	124
Cyprus	0.01	98.3	68.4	0.1	1415	23
Czech Republic	0.16	96.8	57.0	0.5	1079	31

Technical Appendices

Country or region	Share of global population (percent)	Percentage of population above the cutoff	Capacity (percent of GDP)	Share of global RCI (percent)	Average "taxpayer" RCI	Rank by average "taxpayer" RCI
Denmark	0.09	99.8	73.6	0.4	1820	13
Dominican Republic	0.15	26.6	32.9	0.1	149	69
Ecuador	0.21	11.4	24.6	0.0	79	81
Egypt, Arab Rep.	1.15	8.1	7.3	0.1	24	99
El Salvador	0.11	14.8	19.6	0.0	52	87
Eritrea	0.07	0.4	1.2	0.0	1	135
Estonia	0.02	71.0	48.6	0.1	841	36
Ethiopia	1.11	0.0	0.0	0.0	0	156
Finland	0.08	99.6	72.3	0.4	1679	15
France	0.98	98.6	71.2	3.6	1333	25
Gabon	0.02	21.1	27.2	0.0	165	67
Gambia, The	0.02	1.5	3.0	0.0	2	121
Georgia	0.07	3.7	3.4	0.0	10	106
Germany	1.28	96.7	70.2	5.5	1581	18
Ghana	0.34	1.9	2.5	0.0	3	119
Greece	0.17	90.0	62.4	0.5	1097	30
Guatemala	0.2	11.7	17.1	0.0	39	91
Guinea	0.14	3.7	9.5	0.0	8	108
Guinea-Bissau	0.02	0.1	0.2	0.0	0	147
Guyana	0.01	10.6	12.6	0.0	44	90
Haiti	0.13	1.3	3.4	0.0	2	123
Honduras	0.11	7.5	15.4	0.0	30	96
Hungary	0.16	90.8	51.5	0.3	680	40
Iceland	0	99.0	75.8	0.0	1847	11
India	17.02	3.8	3.4	0.3	7	110
Indonesia	3.43	4.6	3.6	0.1	10	107
Iran, Islamic Rep.	1.06	28.8	27.9	0.6	200	62
Iraq	0.41	4.6	5.5	0.0	19	100
Ireland	0.06	98.7	76.9	0.3	1845	12
Israel	0.11	88.5	66.3	0.4	1209	28
Italy	0.91	95.1	69.5	3.3	1333	26
Jamaica	0.04	11.2	25.4	0.0	118	75
Japan	1.99	96.6	70.9	8.1	1504	20
Jordan	0.08	14.8	11.5	0.0	54	85
Kazakhstan	0.24	29.6	21.0	0.1	218	58
Kenya	0.53	0.9	3.5	0.0	2	122
Korea, Dem. Rep.	0.35	0.5	0.8	0.0	2	126
Korea, Rep.	0.75	83.7	61.1	2.1	1029	32
Kuwait	0.04	80.1	68.1	0.2	1816	14
Kyrgyz Republic	0.08	0.4	0.4	0.0	1	134
Lao PDR	0.09	0.7	0.8	0.0	1	138
Latvia	0.04	62.1	42.5	0.0	409	47
Lebanon	0.06	16.0	18.1	0.0	92	78
Lesotho	0.03	7.8	20.2	0.0	19	101
Liberia	0.05	0.1	0.5	0.0	0	141
Libya	0.09	45.3	41.6	0.1	457	46
Lithuania	0.05	69.9	43.6	0.1	465	44
Luxembourg	0.01	100.0	86.0	0.1	4111	1
Macedonia, FYR	0.03	25.1	17.6	0.0	119	74
Madagascar	0.29	0.1	0.5	0.0	0	143
Malawi	0.2	0.1	0.3	0.0	0	149
Malaysia	0.39	39.1	42.7	0.4	362	50
Mali	0.21	0.5	1.9	0.0	1	136
Malta	0.01	86.8	54.5	0.0	784	38
Mauritania	0.05	1.1	1.4	0.0	3	120
Mauritius	0.02	56.5	40.2	0.0	293	54
Mexico	1.6	38.8	42.5	1.4	329	52
Moldova	0.06	1.9	3.0	0.0	8	109

Country or region	Share of global population (percent)	Percentage of population above the cutoff	Capacity (percent of GDP)	Share of global RCI (percent)	Average "taxpayer" RCI	Rank by average "taxpayer" RCI
Mongolia	0.04	1.6	2.6	0.0	7	111
Morocco	0.47	9.9	9.2	0.0	26	97
Mozambique	0.31	0.1	0.2	0.0	0	148
Myanmar	0.79	1.2	3.0	0.0	2	125
Namibia	0.03	18.5	53.8	0.0	196	63
Nepal	0.42	0.7	1.7	0.0	1	132
Netherlands	0.26	99.3	73.5	1.4	2048	7
New Zealand	0.06	91.5	65.7	0.2	1216	27
Nicaragua	0.08	9.4	18.0	0.0	38	92
Niger	0.22	0.1	0.6	0.0	0	142
Nigeria	2.2	0.4	1.2	0.0	1	131
Norway	0.07	99.9	78.2	0.4	1975	8
Oman	0.04	60.7	53.1	0.1	712	39
Pakistan	2.42	0.4	0.3	0.0	1	139
Panama	0.05	24.7	35.7	0.0	240	55
Papua New Guinea	0.09	3.7	7.5	0.0	11	104
Paraguay	0.09	13.2	23.6	0.0	53	86
Peru	0.43	18.5	26.5	0.1	84	80
Philippines	1.29	14.2	18.6	0.2	50	88
Poland	0.59	64.8	43.6	0.9	561	42
Portugal	0.16	80.7	59.8	0.4	819	37
Qatar	0.01	78.6	72.5	0.1	2741	2
Romania	0.34	37.8	25.6	0.2	212	59
Russian Federation	2.22	52.0	29.9	2.3	384	48
Rwanda	0.14	0.3	0.7	0.0	0	140
Saudi Arabia	0.36	61.9	53.9	0.9	894	35
Senegal	0.18	0.1	0.0	0.0	0	150
Serbia and Montenegro	0.12	9.9	3.9	0.0	26	98
Sierra Leone	0.09	0.0	0.0	0.0	0	155
Singapore	0.07	80.5	71.9	0.4	2158	4
Slovak Republic	0.08	84.6	45.4	0.1	621	41
Slovenia	0.03	98.2	59.7	0.1	985	33
Somalia	0.13	0.0	0.1	0.0	0	151
South Africa	0.73	36.1	48.3	1.1	530	43
Spain	0.67	95.1	66.7	2.2	1170	29
Sri Lanka	0.31	5.7	2.9	0.0	6	112
St. Lucia	0	23.7	23.0	0.0	99	77
Sudan	0.56	2.2	5.0	0.0	4	114
Swaziland	0.02	13.4	27.7	0.0	76	83
Sweden	0.14	99.8	72.6	0.5	1402	24
Switzerland	0.12	98.5	75.0	0.5	1496	21
Syrian Arab Republic	0.3	7.6	10.0	0.0	36	93
Taiwan	0.35	94.0	68.9	1.4	1421	22
Tajikistan	0.1	0.0	0.0	0.0	0	152
Tanzania	0.6	0.0	0.0	0.0	0	157
Thailand	1	33.0	29.8	0.5	178	65
Togo	0.1	0.9	2.4	0.0	2	129
Trinidad and Tobago	0.02	52.2	52.1	0.1	976	34
Tunisia	0.16	31.8	26.9	0.1	137	71
Turkey	1.12	30.7	30.5	0.5	177	66
Turkmenistan	0.08	31.1	27.9	0.1	230	56
Uganda	0.45	0.6	1.5	0.0	1	137
Ukraine	0.73	22.6	14.2	0.2	121	73
United Arab Emirates	0.07	79.1	67.2	0.4	1912	9
United Kingdom	0.94	95.7	73.1	4.3	1675	16
United States	4.67	90.5	79.0	34.3	2697	3
Uruguay	0.05	40.2	37.8	0.0	212	60
Uzbekistan	0.41	1.9	4.0	0.0	12	103

Country or region	Share of global population (percent)	Percentage of population above the cutoff	Capacity (percent of GDP)	Share of global RCI (percent)	Average "taxpayer" RCI	Rank by average "taxpayer" RCI
Venezuela, RB	0.41	22.1	23.8	0.2	160	68
Vietnam	1.29	2.7	2.7	0.0	5	113
Yemen, Rep.	0.33	0.0	0.0	0.0	0	158
Zambia	0.18	0.6	3.0	0.0	2	128
Zimbabwe	0.2	4.3	25.4	0.0	46	89
High income	15.61	93.0	73.4	78.5	1845	
Upper middle income	9.3	45.2	39.6	9.6	378	
Lower middle income	38.41	20.1	23.7	11.5	110	
Low income	36.68	2.2	2.9	0.5	4	
Annex I	19.68	80.4	69.5	78.1	1456	
EITs	6.23	41.8	31.7	5.3	309	
LDCs	8.34	0.7	1.8	0.0	1	
EU 15	6.05	96.2	70.6	24.3	1471	
EU +12	1.61	65.2	44.2	2.4	541	
EU 27	7.66	89.7	67.7	26.6	1276	
World	100	27.2	50.3	100.0	367	

7.3 Appendix C: Sensitivity analysis

As we emphasized in the text, any effort to quantify ethical concepts like capacity and responsibility is necessarily subjective, and there can be no "correct" definitions, only more or less reasonable ones. We have attempted to justify our choices, but discussion about alternatives to these parameters is welcome and important. Accordingly, we show in what follows a sensitivity analysis that repeats key output tables with slightly higher or lower values of the key parameters, in particular the development threshold, and the exponents that assign relative weights to responsibility and capacity in the calculation of the RCI.

In Table A3, which is modified from Table 3, we recalculate capacity using a development threshold that is 33 percent lower ($6,000) and 33 percent higher ($12,000) than our reference value of $9,000. Lowering the development threshold excludes fewer people and less income, and thus increases the calculated capacity of low- and middle-income countries relative to high-income countries, while raising the development threshold does the opposite. Even with the lower development threshold, however, the low-income countries, which have 37 percent of global population, still have only 1.2 percent of global capacity; the share of the middle-income countries (48 percent of global population) increases from 21 percent to 25 percent, and the share of the high-income countries decreases from 79 to 74 percent. For an increase of 33 percent in the development threshold, the changes are roughly the same magnitude in the opposite direction.

In Table A4, we show for the same alternative values of the development threshold the share of global RCI, the national bill based on a total mitigation and adaptation expense of 1 percent of GWP, and the average individual bill (based on the share of the population over the development threshold). The countries and country groups shown are the same as in Table 3. The changes have a larger impact in percentage terms on low-income countries, but a larger impact in absolute terms on high-income countries. For instance, changing the development threshold from $9,000 to $6,000

	Low income			Middle income			High income			World		
Global income 2005 ($ trillion PPP)	6			23			33			62		
Share of global income (percent)	9			37			54			100		
Share of population 2005 (percent)	37			48			16			100		
Per capita income 2005 ($ thousands PPP)	2.5			7.4			33.2			9.6		
DEVELOPMENT THRESHOLD	6000	9000	12000	6000	9000	12000	6000	9000	12000	6000	9000	12000
Capacity ($ billion PPP)	0.5	0.2	0.1	9	6	5	27	24	22	37	31	26
Share of global capacity (percent)	1.2	0.5	0.3	25	21	17	74	79	82	100	100	100
Percentage of population over capacity threshold	7.0	2.2	0.8	41	25	16	97	93	86	37	27	21

Table A3. Comparison of capacity, share of global capacity and percentage of population over development threshold for development threshold of $6000, $9000 (reference case), and $12000.

increases the bill to India by roughly 150 percent, though the increase is only $3 billion annually, while it decreases the bill to the United States by only 10 percent, which is about $20 billion annually. The average individual bills vary by a smaller amount in percentage terms, since changing the development threshold changes the number of people over the threshold who are presumed to share the bill. (Recall of course that, while obligations are calculated on a national basis, the average "taxpayer" bill calculation is presented as well, as it reflects the notion that costs should be allocated only among those above the development threshold.)

	Percent of global RCI			Bill at 1 percent of GWP ($ billion PPP adjusted)			Average "taxpayer" bill at 1 percent of GWP ($)		
Development threshold ($ PPP)	**6000**	**9000**	**12000**	**6000**	**9000**	**12000**	**6000**	**9000**	**12000**
United States	31.1	34.3	37.2	192	212	230	664	780	914
EU (27)	25.7	26.6	26.8	159	164	166	336	372	411
United Kingdom	4.0	4.3	4.5	25	26	28	413	458	508
Germany	5.3	5.5	5.6	32	34	35	396	428	464
Russia	3.1	2.3	1.7	19	14	10	172	194	227
Brazil	1.7	1.6	1.5	11	10	9	140	193	257
China	9.0	7.0	5.6	56	43	34	106	142	185
India	0.8	0.3	0.2	5	2	1	38	51	67
South Africa	1.1	1.1	1.0	7	6	6	284	382	498
LDCs	0.1	0.0	0.0	0	0	0	5	7	12
All high income	73.1	78.5	82.3	451	485	508	461	519	585
All middle income	25.9	21.1	17.5	160	130	108	127	170	221
All low income	1.0	0.5	0.2	6	2.8	1	37	55	77
World	100.0	100.0	100.0	617	617	617	257	353	449

Table A4. Comparison of share of global RCI, national bill at 1 percent of GWP, and per capita bill at 1 percent of GWP (based on fraction of population over development threshold) for development threshold of $6,000, $9,000 (reference case), and $12,000.

We have chosen an intuitively reasonable expression, $R^a C^b$, for combining R and C into an RCI. It allows for choosing different weighting of R and C. It is familiar to economists (where it is known as Cobb-Douglas production function). It satisfies the critical condition that RCIs are consistently defined whether you're looking at countries, fractions of countries, or individuals, since the sum of the RCIs calculated for parts (say nations within a region) is equal to the RCI of the whole. And, it is a simple and analytically straightforward form. Still, there are other formulas that could conceivably be used to combine *R* and *C* into an RCI. However, we suspect that ultimately the choice of weightings for responsibility and capacity captures most of the meaningful variation in possible function forms. So, in the final table (Table A5), we explore alternative values for the weightings. We show the same output as in Table A4 (share of global RCI, national and per capita bills), but this time with three possible weightings *a* and *b*.

In our reference case, capacity was weighted higher than responsibility, with exponents of 0.6 and 0.4 respectively; in the sensitivity analysis we show a case with greater weighting of capacity (0.8, v. 0.2 for responsibility), and a case with a greater weighting on responsibility (0.4 for capacity v. 0.6 for responsibility).

	Percent of global RCI			Bill at 1 percent of GWP ($ billion PPP adjusted)			Average individual bill at 1 % of GWP ($)		
Capacity weighting	**0.8**	**0.6**	**0.4**	**0.8**	**0.6**	**0.4**	**0.8**	**0.6**	**0.4**
Responsibility weighting	**0.2**	**0.4**	**0.6**	**0.2**	**0.4**	**0.6**	**0.2**	**0.4**	**0.6**
United States	33.1	34.3	35.4	205	212	219	753	780	804
EU (27)	27.8	26.6	25.4	172	164	157	389	372	355
United Kingdom	4.5	4.3	4.1	28	26	25	481	458	432
Germany	5.6	5.5	5.5	34	34	34	432	428	423
Russia	1.9	2.3	2.9	12	14	18	156	194	240
Brazil	1.8	1.6	1.4	11	10	9	221	193	168
China	7.1	7.0	6.9	44	43	43	143	142	140
India	0.4	0.3	0.3	2	2	2	57	51	47
South Africa	0.9	1.1	1.2	6	6	7	338	382	433
LDCs	0.0	0.0	0.0	0	0	0	10	7	5
All high income	78.7	78.5	78.1	486	485	482	520	519	517
All middle income	20.8	21.1	21.5	129	130	133	168	170	173
All low income	0.5	0.5	0.4	3.0	2.8	2.5	60	55	50
World	100.0	100.0	100.0	617	617	617	353	353	353

Table A5. Comparison of share of global RCI, national bill at 1 percent of GWP, and average individual bill at 1 percent of GWP (based on fraction of population over development threshold) for capacity/responsibility weighting of 0.8/0.2, 0.6/0.4 (reference case) and 0.4/0.6.

The results show that, in general, these changes in the weighting of responsibility and capacity make substantially less difference than the changes in the development threshold. The notable exception is Russia, which, because it has very low capacity relative to its responsibility, is relatively sensitive to the parameter choice. This is an important example of the general case, which is that the weighting of responsibility vs. capacity matters only to countries that are much higher on one than the other.

7.4 Appendix D: Emissions trajectories and risk analysis

The risk calculations shown in Section 2 are based on the Monte Carlo Climate Model (MC^2) built by Paul Baer and Michael Mastrandrea, and used in the 2006 report "High Stakes: Designing Emissions Trajectories to Reduce the Risk of Dangerous Climate Change" published by the Institute for Public Policy Research in the United Kingdom. It contains a far more detailed discussion of both the model and the results than this appendix.

7.4.1 About Monte Carlo models

Monte Carlo models are so-called because their results, rather than being a single number, are reported as a probability distribution – like the expected results of a game of, say, roulette. Briefly, each uncertain variable in the model is input as a probability distribution, and a computer's random-number generator is used to select a value from that distribution each time the model is run. When the model is run repeatedly (typically hundreds or thousands of times), the output value or values will sometimes be higher than the mean result and sometimes lower, depending on which input values were selected on each run by the random number generator. The full set of output values form a probability distribution, which can be interpreted as representing the likelihood that the "real world" outcome will actually be a particular value. Thus we can say, for a hypothetical emissions scenario, that if 50 percent of the model runs resulted in a temperature increase over 2°C, then the "risk" of exceeding 2°C that is associated with that scenario is 50 percent.

Such results need to be interpreted with great caution. Crucially, the uncertainty in the input variables in a model like the simple climate model does not only reflect the stochastic (random) processes in the climate system, but also (and in fact primarily) ignorance about the climate system. The uncertainty in, say, the climate sensitivity (the equilibrium warming expected in response to a doubling of CO_2 concentration), is not like the uncertainty of a gambling result. When we say that there is (for example) a 10 percent likelihood that the climate sensitivity is more than 4.5°C, we do not mean that, if we doubled the CO_2 concentration 100 times, it would be over 4.5°C 10 of those times; or that if we doubled the CO_2 on 100 earthlike planets, it would be over 4.5°C 10 of those times. Rather, the estimate is a "subjective probability": an estimate, made by a human (or a group of humans) that, based on all the evidence, it is about as likely that the climate sensitivity is more than 4.5°C that (for example) you would draw a black ball from an urn for which we have various forms of evidence suggesting it contains 10 black and 90 white balls.

For properties of complex systems like the climate, the various forms of evidence about the climate sensitivity (or the response of the carbon cycle to warming, or the radiative forcing of aerosols) do not very strongly constrain the likely values. (To continue the ball-and-urn metaphor, some experts might interpret the evidence to say the urn has 10 black balls, but some conclude a few more, and some a few less.) That is, different experts can quite reasonably hold different beliefs about the probability distributions of the critical variables. Thus, there is not and cannot be a "correct" probability distribution, since it is a measure of our remaining ignorance about the climate system, rather than a well-known property of the climate system itself. As a consequence, it is appropriate to report the output of probabilistic models such as MC^2 as a range that accounts for the spread in the interpretations of the evidence. For this reason, we report the "likelihood of exceeding 2°C" of our emissions pathways as a range (for example, between 17 and 36 percent for our most stringent trajectory) that reasonably, if approximately, captures the range of reasonable scientific opinion.

A further discussion of the implications of this "multi-dimensional uncertainty" is beyond our scope. The critical point is that, while different models using different assumptions will produce different likelihoods, there is a *reasonable* overlap, which gives guidance about broad risk estimates for exceeding 2°C. Ultimately, decisions then need to be based on ethical judgments about risk aversion (including consideration of the distribution of risk), not on an appeal to science as such.

7.4.2 The structure of the MC^2 model

MC^2 is a simple parameterized climate model which calculates the annual change in global mean temperature based on the difference between the current temperature and the "implied equilibrium temperature" – that is, the temperature that would be reached at equilibrium if radiative forcing were held constant from that point out. Radiative forcing, in turn, is calculated as the sum of forcing from CO_2, the offsetting forcing from aerosols, and a single specified forcing from "other non-CO_2 gases". The emissions trajectory for CO_2 is specified by the user, and the change in CO_2 concentrations is determined by the difference between emissions and the uptake of carbon by the global carbon sink.

The behavior of the model is governed by five variables which are treated as uncertain, for which a different value is randomly drawn from a specified probability distribution in each run of the model. The five uncertain variables are the climate sensitivity, the effective thermal inertia of the ocean, the initial value of land-use emissions (which also defines the initial carbon sink), the rate of change of the carbon sink and the initial value of aerosol forcing. In the default configuration of the model, normal distributions are used for each of the uncertain variables except the climate sensitivity; the input probability for the climate sensitivity can be chosen from a set of six that have been published in the scientific literature. (There are other even more "extreme" probability distributions published, but we believe these six span most of the range of the estimates that would be considered reasonable by experts.) And while the model is built from simple equations for temperature and the carbon cycle, it produces a reasonable reproduction of the range of results from the most complex coupled global general circulation models.

For a given configuration of input probability distributions, the model is then run several hundred times for the period from 2000 to 2100, generating a distribution of output results for the peak temperature over that time period. As noted above, if (say) 20 of 200 runs result in a peak temperature over 2°C, we report that the specified scenario has a 10 percent risk of exceeding the 2°C threshold. The variation reported in our results – for example, a 17 to 36 percent risk for the lowest emissions scenario – is based on a run where the probability distribution for the climate sensitivity is fixed at either the most "optimistic" of the six (the log-normal distribution of Wigley and Raper 2001) or the most "pessimistic" (the distribution of Murphy et al. 2005, based on their own Monte Carlo analysis using the Hadley Centre's GCM).

For further information, see Baer and Mastrandrea (2006), or contact Paul Baer (pbaer@ecoquity.org).

Acknowledgements

Greenhouse Development Rights has been long in the making, and there are many to thank. The first is Steve Bernow, now deceased, who helped the authors launch the "Per Capita Plus" effort (to develop an emissions rights-based framework that could take account of differing national circumstances) which by its failure set up Greenhouse Development Rights. The second is Andrew Pendleton at Christian Aid, now a close colleague, who has provided us with invaluable financial as well as moral/political support. Jörg Haas at the Heinrich Böll Foundation has since put his shoulder to this wheel as well, and by so doing has significantly increased the robustness of this effort. We also acknowledge the support of the Climate Policy Research Program (CLIPORE) of Mistra, the Foundation for Strategic Environmental Research.

We would also like to thank Simon Rettallack of the UK's Institute for Public Policy Research for his support of the risk-analysis research that underlies our climate scenarios.

On another front, there is Eric Kemp-Benedict at the Stockholm Environment Institute in Boston, who has developed the GDRs calculator and otherwise been a huge help in all sorts of quantitative, methodological and data-related matters, John Gershman at the Wagner School of Public Policy, who has added some critical expertise on civil-society governance issues, Kate Raworth from the Oxfam International Research Department, whose sharp eye and keen wits have been of tremendous help in ways both large and small, and finally Matthew Lockwood of the UK's Institute for Public Policy Research and Charlie Kronick from UK Greenpeace, for detailed and extremely useful critical readings of earlier versions of this report.

We also want to acknowledge the climate movement itself, the Climate Action Network in particular, without which we probably would not even have been able to conceive of this effort, not properly in any case, and Friends of the Earth International, for its diffuse but indispensable solidarity.

References

Agarwal, A., and S. Narain. 1991. *Global Warming in an Unequal World: A Case of Environmental Colonialism.* New Delhi: Centre for Science and Environment.

Agarwal, A., S. Narain, and A. Sharma, eds. 1999. *Green Politics: Global Environmental Negotiations 1.* New Delhi: Centre for Science and the Environment.

Azar, C., and S. H. Schneider. 2002. "Are the economic costs of stabilising the atmosphere prohibitive?" *Ecological Economics* 42(1–2): pp 73–80.

Azar, C., K. Lindgren, E. Larson, and K. Mollersten. 2006. "Carbon capture and storage from fossil fuels and biomass – Costs and potential role in stabilizing the atmosphere." *Climatic Change* 74(1–3): pp 47–79.

Baer, P., and T. Athanasiou. 2007. *A brief, adequacy and equity-based evaluation of some prominent climate policy frameworks and proposals.* 2007 Heinrich Böll Foundation Global Issue Paper. http://www.boell.de/index.html?http://www.boell.de/en/04_thema/5055.html&lang=en

Baer, P., and M. Mastrandrea. 2006. *High Stakes: Designing emissions pathways to reduce the risk of dangerous climate change.* London: Institute for Public Policy Research. http://www.ippr.org.

Barclays Capital. 2007. *Equity Gilt Study 2007.* London: Barclays Bank.

Climate Action Network International. 2007. "Indicative ranges of emission reduction objectives for Annex 1 countries." Submission to the AWG (Ad Hoc Working Group on Further Commitments for Annex I Parties under the Kyoto Protocol). June.

Cowell, F. A. 1996. *Measuring Inequality.* Second edition. London: Prentice Hall.

Criqui, P., and N. Kouvaritakis. 2000. "World energy projections to 2030." *International Journal of Global Energy Issues,* 14(1–4): pp 116–136.

DeCanio, S. J. 2003. *Economic Models of Climate Change: A Critique.* New York: Palgrave MacMillan.

Den Elzen, M. G. J., and M. Meinshausen. 2005. *Meeting the EU 2°C Climate Target: Global and Regional Emission Implications.* Netherlands Environment Agency, Report 72800103.

Hansen, J., M. Sato, R. Ruedy, et al. 2007. "Dangerous human-made interference with climate: a GISS modelE study." *Atmospheric Chemistry And Physics* 7(9): pp 2287–2312.

Hansen, J., M. Sato, R. Ruedy, et al. 2006. "Global temperature change." Proceedings of The National Academy of Sciences of The United States of America 103(39): pp 14288–14293.

IPCC. 2000. N. Nakicenovic, and R Swart, eds. *Emissions Scenarios: Special Report of the Intergovernmental Panel on Climate Change.* Cambridge, UK: Cambridge University Press.

Kemp-Benedict, E. 2001. "Income Distribution and Poverty: Methods for Using Available Data in Global Analysis." PoleStar Technical Note #4. http://gdrs.sourceforge.net/docs/PoleStar_TechNote_4.pdf.

Lohmann, L., et al. 2006. *Carbon trading, a critical conversation on climate change, privatization and power.* Development dialog #48. England: Dog Hammarskjöld Center, Uppsala Sweden and the Corner House (http://www.cornerhouse.org.uk).

Lopez, H. 2006. "A normal relationship? Poverty, growth, inequality." A World Bank Policy Research Working Paper. http://econ.worldbank.org/external/default/main?pagePK=64165259&theSitePK= 469372& piPK=64165421&menuPK=64166093&entityID=000016406_20060110164713.

Meinshausen, M. 2006. *On the Risk of Overshooting 2°C. Avoiding Dangerous Climate Change.* H. J. Schellnhuber, W. Cramer, N. Nakicenovic, T. Wigley, and G, Yohe. Cambridge, UK: Cambridge University Press.

Müller, B. 2002. *Equity in Climate Change: The Great Divide.* EV 31. Oxford: Oxford Institute for Energy Studies. September 31.

Oxfam Briefing Paper 104. 2007. "Adapting to climate change: What's needed in poor countries, and who should pay." May 29. http://www.oxfam.org/en/files/bp104_climate_change_0705.pdf/download.

Pacala, S., and R. Socolow. 2004. "Stabilization wedges: Solving the climate problem for the next 50 years with current technologies." *Science* 305: pp 968–972.

Pritchett, L. 2003. "Who is not poor? Proposing a higher international standard for poverty." The Center for Global Development, 21(1): pp 1–23. http://www.cgdev.org/content/publications/detail/2758.

Pritchett, L. 2006. "Who is not poor? Dreaming of a world truly free of poverty." *The World Bank Research Observer.* Working Paper Number 33. November. http://wbro.oxfordjournals.org/cgi/reprint/lkj002?ijkey=nfo6au5gH8Lhprd&keytype=ref.

Scientific Expert Group on Climate Change. 2007. *Confronting Climate Change: Avoiding the Unmanageable, Managing the Unavoidable.* Research Triangle Park. Sigma Xi and the United Nations Foundation.

Shue, H. 1993. "Subsistence emissions and luxury emissions." *Law and Policy* 15(1): pp 39–59.

Simms, A., J. Magrath, and H. Reid. 2004. *Up in Smoke.* London: New Economics Foundation. http://www.neweconomics.org/gen/z_sys_publicationdetail.aspx?pid=196.

Stern, N. 2006. *The Stern Review on the Economics of Climate Change.* London: UK Government Economic Service. http://www.sternreview.org.uk.

UNFCCC secretariat. 2007. Analysis of existing and planned investment and financial flows relevant to the development of effective and appropriate international response to climate change. http://unfccc.int/files/cooperation_and_support/financial_mechanism/application/pdf/background_paper.pdf.

Endnotes

1 By "aggressive realist scenarios" we mean, for example, the recommendations of the Scientific Expert Group (2007) or the Stern Review (2006), both of which put 450 ppm CO_2-equivalent as their lowest recommended stabilization target. Yet both acknowledge (following for example Meinshausen 2006) that 450 ppm CO_2-equivalent has at best even odds of keeping below 2°C warming, and something like a 20 percent likelihood of exceeding 3°C warming. And as James Hansen and colleagues (2006, 2007) among others have warned, the destabilization of the Greenland Ice Sheet is possible even before global mean warming reaches the 2°C level, potentially causing up to seven meters of sea level rise, over centuries or, perhaps, much more quickly. Although there are many other potential impacts that would count as regionally or even globally catastrophic, the threat of destabilizing the ice sheets seems for obvious reasons to be a critical justification for urgent precaution.

2 See Meinshausen (2006), or Baer and Mastrandrea (2006).

3 As we discuss later, even if Annex 1 countries reached 80 percent below 1990 levels by 2050 through exclusively *domestic* reductions and, at the same time, non-Annex 1 emissions converged to equal them (in per capita terms), global emissions would still be inconsistent with a high likelihood of staying below 2°C. Worse, in most "realist" proposals, steep Annex 1 reductions are not assumed to be exclusively domestic, but rather to be met, in large part, with purchased offsets.

4 This must be done, of course, even as the impacts of the now inevitable warming intensify the development burden and undercut efforts to alleviate poverty. The disproportionate impact of climate change on poor people and developing countries due to both specific climatic impacts and greater vulnerability is well documented in the report of Working Group II of the IPCC's Fourth Assessment Report. A more political view of the topic, and in particular its likely impacts on development progress and poverty alleviation, can be found in, for example, "Up In Smoke" (Simms et al., 2004) from the New Economics Foundation (http://www.neweconomics.org).

5 See, for example, Barclay Capital's "Equity Gilt Study 2007," which argues for the optimistic case with these words: "If ever the time were ripe for such an energy revolution, it is now. And like all historical adoptions of general purpose technologies, the process should prove immensely stimulative to economic growth. Oddly, the climate change policy debate is couched in terms of the cost to GDP growth. Even the proponents of policy shifts tend to assume a negative effect on growth. This stance is underselling the actual impact of an energy revolution. All of the historical changes in energy supply – from dung to wood to coal to oil – were stimulative for the economy concerned. Every major technological change was accompanied or followed by faster economic growth." We accept this argument, but believe that it tells far less than the whole story.

6 Per capita approaches are strongly identified with the "Contraction and Convergence" approach. This is as it should be, for C&C was the first real "equity reference framework," and as such it has done a great deal to publicly establish the need for just global burden-sharing as an essential aspect of an emergency climate stabilization program. It has acquired, and deserves, a great deal of respect and support. (We used to be C&C supporters ourselves.) But the simplicity that is one of its great virtues is also one of its greatest weaknesses. More particularly, in its focus on equality of emissions rights, it loses sight of the *end* to which emissions rights can only be a *means* – sustainable human development for all, even in this a world that is profoundly constrained by the prior overuse of the now-scarce atmospheric commons. Our analysis has convinced us that, under stringent mitigation targets, C&C cannot deliver this essential *developmental equity*, and it is to respond to this requirement that we have been elaborating the GDRs framework.

C&C fails to deliver developmental equity for two fundamental reasons. First, it fails to account for the historical advantage acquired by the developed countries, who had decades of unrestrained emissions. Second, it fails to account for the wide range of variation in national circumstances, particularly among developing countries but also among high emitting "industrialized" countries, many of which (like Russia) are now quite poor.

Supporters of C&C have variously argued that these drawbacks are sufficiently minor that they can be ignored, or that modifications can be made to C&C's basic allocation scheme to improve its "performance" on these issues. We considered these arguments carefully and over a long period of time, and concluded that it would be far better to take the South at its word, and to work toward a viable global climate stabilization framework with "the right to development" rather than the "equal per capita emissions rights" that C&C (implicitly) posits as its proxy. Our argument, in a nutshell, is that this "developmental equity," and not instead of emissions equity, must be the organizing principle of a viable climate framework.

We have elaborated these criticisms in a framework comparison for the Heinrich Böll Foundation (Baer and Athanasiou, 2007), and intend to eventually publish a more detailed analysis of C&C and per capita approaches more generally.

7 The UNFCCC famously notes in its preamble that "the global nature of climate change calls for the widest possible cooperation by all countries and their participation in an effective and appropriate international response, in accordance with their common but differentiated responsibilities and respective capabilities and their social and economic conditions."

8 The three scenarios are based on CO_2 emissions only, including both fossil fuel emissions and land use emissions. All three scenarios begin with historical fossil fuel emissions through 2005 and estimated land use emissions of 1.5 GtC/yr. Emissions after 2005 are projected to rise at 2.5 percent a year until 2010, 2009 and 2007 respectively, at which point the rate of increase starts to decline. All three trajectories peak in 2015, before declining by 2050 to 50, 65 and 80 percent below 1990 levels (estimated at 7.5 GtC including land use emissions). The annual rate of emissions reductions reach a peak rate of 3.4, 4.4 and 6.0 percent respectively. Non-CO_2 emissions are assumed to fall such that the radiative forcing from non-CO_2 GHGs declines by 50 percent between 2010 and 2050 (from 1 Wm^{-2} to 0.5 Wm^{-2}).

	Reductions start	Emissions peak	2050 CO_2 emissions relative to 1990	Maximum rate of reductions	Chance of exceeding 2°C	Peak concentration ppm (Co2/CO2-eq)
Trajectory 1 (least stringent)	2010	2015	50% below	3.4%/yr	26–55%	445/500
Trajectory 2	2009	2015	65% below	4.4%/yr	21–46%	435/485
Trajectory 3 (most stringent)	2007	2015	80% below	6.0%/yr	17–36%	425/470

9 These calculations are based on the model used in Baer and Mastrandrea (2006), cited in Note 2. Because the probability distributions for key parameters such as the climate sensitivity and the behavior of the carbon cycle are not well defined, the probabilistic methodology takes as an input subjective expert opinion about the uncertainty of various parameters. This method accounts for the fact that a range of reasonable assumptions can be made about key parameters by reporting the calculated risk as a range (in which the upper and lower bounds reflect the spread in the scientific opinion). For a discussion of the issues and the model used in these calculations, see the appendix, or Baer and Mastrandrea (2006).

10 There is no universal definition of "CO_2-equivalent levels." The Stern Review recently established the precedent of referring to the equivalent concentration levels of the Kyoto gases only, and the 470 ppm CO_2-equivalent figure given for this trajectory is calculated on this basis for the purpose of comparison. However, more precisely CO_2-equivalent levels should include all radiative forcings, positive and negative, as that is what produces the overall impact on the climate system. The largest additional forcing is the negative forcing from aerosols. In our model, aerosol forcings reduce the net radiative forcing to about 435 ppm CO_2-e at the peak.

11 Perhaps there are even more radical trajectories, in which global emissions actually go negative. These might be possible with "negative emission" mitigation options, such as biomass-based power coupled with carbon capture and sequestration (Azar et al. 2006), which extract carbon dioxide from the atmosphere. (Coal-based power coupled with sequestration could be close to zero emission, but not negative.) This could open the door to trajectories with higher probabilities of preserving the 2°C line than the most stringent of our emergency trajectories. In theory, it could also open the door to trajectories that slightly delay the necessary emissions peak. In practice, however, such trajectories would require us to bank on debatable assumptions: that we would eventually find these unproven technologies to be feasible, that we would implement them at a sufficiently large scale to reverse our earlier delay, that we would deploy them rapidly enough to avoid a climate catastrophe in the meantime. It is one thing to *hope* that these will prove true, and thus improve our chances of keeping within 2°C. It is quite another to *assume* that they will prove true, and then use that assumption to justify a sluggish response now. For this reason, we choose to take these options off the table for the purposes of our discussion.

12 Hansen, James. 2006. "Climate Change: On the Edge." (*The Independent*, February 17, 2006). The details of Hansen's analysis can be found in James Hansen, Makiko Sato, et. al., 2006.

13 Climate Action Network International, 2007.

14 Scientific Expert Group, 2007.

15 Note, however, that the Stern Review focused on stabilization scenarios, while our scenarios are projected to *reduce* concentrations after their peak. In practice our ability to reduce after peaking will depend not only on our resolve and technical capability but also on carbon-cycle feedbacks beyond our control.

16 See the IPCC's Fourth Assessment Report, Summary for Policy Makers of the report of Working Group III, Table SPM-4.

17 The SRES B1 scenario is characterized by relatively low population growth, "reductions in material intensity, and the introduction of clean and resource-efficient technologies" (IPCC, 2000) at aggressive rates that exceed historic precedent. And like all the SRES reference scenarios, it includes by definition no explicit climate policy.

18 The reader may notice that this way of presenting the problem is actually quite optimistic, in that it implicitly posits that northern emissions magically and entirely disappear by 2020, making the entire precautionary emissions budget available to the South. Without this assumption, southern emissions would have to start their precipitous decline even earlier – well before 2020.

19 The SRES B1 scenario has southern per capita income rising at a rate of around 4.5 percent per year. Using this rate, per capita income in the South would thus have not quite doubled from the 2005 average of around $4,800 (PPP adjusted) to around $9,400 in 2020.

20 Stern argued, more precisely, that spending 1 percent of GWP would save us damages equivalent to between 5 and 20 percent. This cost estimate, however, was associated with a concentration target in the range of 500 to 550 CO_2-equivalent, which is far more likely to yield 3°C than 2°C of warming, as Stern himself admits.

21 This is not to imply that poor people are responsible for all or even most land clearing, as opposed to national or international elites; only that land-use emissions must be dramatically reduced, whatever their purpose.

22 All dollar figures in this paper are given using 2005 US dollars, converted on a purchasing power parity (PPP) basis.

23 According to Pritchett (2003) the use of this line "is justifiable, more consistent with international fairness, and is a better foundation for the World Bank's organizational mission of poverty reduction." See also Pritchett (2006).

24 Jo Johnson, "Worlds collide in India over global warming," *Financial Times*, June 7, 2007.

25 Bill Gates is still listed as the world's richest man in the March 2007 Forbes list of billionaires. However, that title is now held by telecom tycoon Carlos Slim. A Mexican, Slim is a citizen of a country that is not even in the top 50 in terms of per capita national income. ("Mexican tycoon overtakes Bill Gates as world's richest man," by Fiona Walsh, *London Guardian*, July 3, 2007.)

26 And of course the Brazilian proposal famously allocated obligations, albeit only within Annex I, on the basis of responsibility for global temperature change.
27 Plainly deforestation causes a large fraction of the emissions from tropical countries today. Yet most northern countries were largely deforested centuries ago for the same reasons – for timber, fuel-wood and agriculture. By one calculation that we have done, per capita emissions from land use change in the United States reached 10 tons of carbon (not CO_2!) per capita in the mid-19th century. But these forests are now regrowing, perhaps fertilized by increased CO_2 concentrations, and even being claimed as carbon-sinks. Clearly a fair treatment of land-use emissions will require consideration of these issues.
28 This distinction between luxury and subsistence emissions has been popularized by Anil Agarwal and Sunita Narain (1991; see also Agarwal, Narain and Sharma 1999) of India's Centre for Science and the Environment, and by the philosopher Henry Shue (1993).
29 Benito Müller (2002) is quite good, and equally brief.
30 We use here the so-called "log-normal distribution" as a model of the income distribution with two country-specific parameters: the mean per capita income and the Gini coefficient. For an explanation, see the technical appendix. For a justification of the use of log-normals for income distributions, see for example Lopez (2006).
31 Note that the fact that the chart appears to reach a maximum income level at about $20,000 does not mean that there are not people in India with higher incomes. It is rather that the average income of the highest 1 percent is still fairly low.
32 This observation might seem counter-intuitive to readers who note that Unfairland has not only more capacity than Fairland, but also more development need. Actually, this fact merely underscores the importance of sharing the national burden equitably among citizens; that is, sharing it among the wealthy citizens who have the capacity to pay it. The capacity-based tax will not be a burden on the poor of Unfairland so long as it is not passed down to them, but rather absorbed by the wealthy of Unfairland, on whose capacity it is based.
33 The World Bank defines countries by income class using per capita income in market exchange rate, not purchasing power parity, terms. The official classes (in 2005 dollars) are low income (below $875), lower-middle ($876–$3,465), upper middle ($3,466–$10,725) and high (over $10,725). We combine lower-middle and upper-middle income groups. In PPP terms, the borders are on the order of $2,000, $7,000, and $15,000. For a list of countries, see the Appendix.
34 For an approach that is similar to ours in spirit, but significantly different in details, see Oxfam (2007).
35 The UNFCCC secretariat's background paper (UNFCCC secretariat, 2007) argues that that "global additional investment and financial flows of USD 200–210 billion will be necessary in 2030 to return GHG emissions to current levels," and that this amount "is large compared with the funding currently available under the Convention and its Kyoto Protocol, but small in relation to estimated global gross domestic product (GDP) (0.3-0.5 percent) and global investment (1.1–1.7 percent) in 2030."
36 Some models simply calculate the reduction in GWP v. a baseline in (say) 2050; others estimate a marginal and average cost of emissions reductions and a total amount of reductions to calculate a total cost.
37 For example, many economic models assume that as energy prices rise with carbon prices, central banks will respond with anti-inflationary measures, causing significant losses in GDP. There are many reasons to think such measures would be inappropriate. For further discussion, see, for example, *Economic Models of Climate Change: A Critique* by Stephen J. DeCanio (2003).
38 The global adaptation need will be even more challenging to calculate than a global mitigation shortfall, for the scope of adaptations reflect choices that are fundamentally social and not economic in nature. But this challenge is by no means unique to the GDRs approach. Any approach that takes the notion of "polluter pays" seriously requires a cost assessment. To a first order, this assessment can be envisioned as an evolution and generalization of the process that is already underway to develop National Adaptation Plans of Action. See also section 5 of (UNFCCC secretariat, 2007).
39 Because each country's share of global RCI is not the same as its share of GWP, a practical proposal to raise 1 percent (or some other specific fraction) of GWP in taxes paid to an international fund would require appropriate scaling. We thank Kate Raworth of Oxfam for pointing this out.

40 See for example "Bush's New Defense Budget," by Robert Higgs, February 14, 2005: "The Pentagon's own budget – for fiscal year 2006, the widely reported amount of $419 billion in discretionary budget authority – does not include the costs of nuclear warheads, which the Department of Energy produces; the defense-related activities of the Department of State, including "foreign military financing"; the past military services being compensated currently by benefits provided through the Department of Veterans Affairs; the defense-related activities of the Homeland Security Department, such as the Coast Guard's defense activities; various defense-related activities of several other federal departments; or the current interest costs of previous, debt-financed military activities. Applying my rule of thumb, I estimate that the government's total military-related outlays in fiscal year 2006 will be in the neighborhood of $840 billion – or, approximately a third of the total budget, as opposed to the 16 percent that one calculates by comparing the Pentagon's $419 billion request to the administration's total request, $2.57 trillion." Posted at http://www.independent.org/newsroom/article.asp?id=1464

41 GWP is $46 trillion and military expenditures are $1.2 trillion in 2006 (or approximately 2.5 percent). See http://www.sipri.org/contents/milap/milex/mex_trends.html and en.wikipedia.org/wiki/World_economy.

42 Christian Azar and Steve Schneider (2002) among others have pointed out that in a world of continuing economic growth at 2 or 3 percent annually, even a 5 percent decrease in GWP in 2050 implies only a delay of two years or so in becoming twice as wealthy. Presumably, most people, if asked whether they would go without raises for two years in order to preserve the planet for their grandchildren, would not hesitate.

43 Adaptation is, at its core, a problem of resilience and adaptive capacity, and thus a development challenge that cannot plausibly be addressed by market-based institutions. So while modeling the mitigation side of a global climate regime makes good sense, and while market institutions are certain to play a role in the mitigation regime, adaptation investments must, for fundamental reasons, be implemented through democratically controlled funds that rely heavily on the involvement of civil society.

44 Based on the global growth rates for CO_2 emissions specified in the IPCC's SRES A1B scenario.

45 Our "no regrets" trajectory uses growth rates in per capita emissions from the SRES B1 scenario as a plausible guess. The result – 1.3 GtC of no regrets reductions below the A1B scenario in 2025 – is very close to the estimate based on bottom-up calculations in the IPCC's AR4 Working Group III Summary for Policymakers, which reports about 1.5–2 GtC of no regrets reductions below A1B in 2030. We suspect that the actual opportunity may be much larger, particularly if policies are designed intelligently and as technological advances bring costs down, but it will still only be a modest part of the necessary "emergency program."

46 Pacala and Socolow (2004).

47 Note that China's reduction obligation for the whole 2011-2025 period is proportional to its share of global RCI based on 2005 figures. If its RCI were recalculated in an intermediate year its share would presumably be somewhat larger.

48 See, most exhaustively, Lohmann et. al. (2006).

49 Given that, in recent years, global emissions have exceeded those projected in all SRES scenarios, it is benign indeed.

50 Based on World Bank data (per capita growth rates and per capita income through 2006).

51 Baer and Athanasiou (2007). See, in particular, the discussion of the South-North Dialogue's "Equity in the Greenhouse" proposal.

52 Climate Action Network International (2007).

53 "Participation thresholds are based on a Capability–Responsibility index (for example, Criqui and Kouvaritakis, 2000), and is defined as the sum of per capita GDP income (in PPP €1,000 per capita), which relates to the capability to act, and of per capita CO_2-equivalent emissions (in tCO_2 per capita), reflecting the responsibility in climate change." Den Elzen and Meinshausen (2005), cited in Climate Action Network International (2007).

54 Al Gore, "Moving Beyond Kyoto," *The New York Times*, July 1, 2007.

55 Quoted in Peter Foster, "India snubs West on climate change," *UK Telegraph*, December 6, 2006.

THE AUTHORS

Paul Baer is an internationally recognized expert on issues of equity and climate change, with training in ecological economics, ethics, philosophy of science, risk analysis and simulation modeling. He completed his PhD in 2005 at UC Berkeley's Energy and Resources Group; his dissertation examined the interconnection between equity, risk and scientific uncertainty – three topics at the heart of the climate problem. He also has a BA in Economics from Stanford University and a Masters in Environmental Planning and Management from Louisiana State University. He recently completed a post-doctoral research fellowship at Stanford University's Center for Environmental Science and Policy, addressing the interaction of climate change and forest fire in Alaska. He is currently the Research Director for EcoEquity (http://www.ecoequity.org), a climate-advocacy organization he co-founded in 2000 with Tom Athanasiou, with whom he also co-authored the 2002 book *Dead Heat: Global Justice and Global Warming* (Seven Stories Press). His recent work includes *High Stakes: Designing Emissions Pathways to Reduce the Risk of Dangerous Climate Change* (with Mike Mastrandrea, published by the Institute for Public Policy Research).

Tom Athanasiou is a long-time left Green, a former software engineer, a technology critic and, most recently, a climate justice activist. His interests have wandered from the nature and limits of artificial intelligence technology to, most recently, injustice as, in itself, a wellspring of ecological crisis. Tom is the author of *Divided Planet: The Ecology of Rich and Poor* and the co-author of *Dead Heat: Global Justice and Global Warming*. In the late 1990s, Tom began to focus on global climate justice. In 2000, with Paul Baer, he founded EcoEquity, an activist think tank focused on the development and promotion of fair and potentially viable approaches to emergency climate stabilization. This work has taken shape as the Greenhouse Development Rights Framework. Tom is now the director of EcoEquity. In his spare time, he is developing a new book, the working title of which is *A New Deal for the Greenhouse Century*.

Sivan Kartha is a Senior Scientist at the Stockholm Environment Institute whose research and publications pertain to climate change and sustainable development. He is Director of SEI's Climate and Energy Program, focusing on equity and efficiency in the formation of an international climate regime, and has worked with policymakers, private sector actors, foundations and NGOs in countries throughout the world. Sivan also works on the environmental and socioeconomic impacts of the burgeoning biofuel economy in developing countries.